W0035986

Advance Praise

Genius is simple. Innovation is simple. It lies at the confluence of selfish interest and selfless interest. Dr Kaustubh Dhargalkar rightly calls it 'enlightened self-interest'. Set precepts and theories of business are in a state of flux in times that are dramatically changing. Obsolescence is constantly snapping at the heels of innovation. In such times, Dhargalkar propounds a path that unfolds like the layers of a simple onion peel, deeper, yet deeper, till, at the core, we encounter the jewel of human connectivity. Empathy. Vasudhaiva Kutumbakam.

Amish Tripathi, *Diplomat, Columnist and Author of bestsellers* The Immortals of Meluha, The Secret of the Nagas, The Oath of the Vayuputras, Ram: Scion of Ikshvaku, Sita: Warrior of Mithila *and* Raavan: Enemy of Aryavarta

Dr Kaustubh provides a practical guide to innovation.

Dr Vijay Govindarajan, *Coxe Distinguished Professor at Tuck School of Business at Dartmouth College;* New York Times *and* Wall Street Journal *Bestselling Author*

Simple, lucid, engaging, insightful … *a whack on the head … opens up horizons of invaluable possibilities.* Kaustubh's fantastic narration challenges every mind to seek beyond the constraints, opens up untapped reserves and follows through by actually showing how to make it possible. It unleashes terrific unexplored value and potential!!

Kush Kamra, *Chairman and MD—GOSC, Metlife Insurance*

This book is a must read for all entrepreneurs and intrapreneurs. The case studies chosen are very relatable and insightful that bring out the nuances of business model innovation. Provides a clear, non-jargonistic and applicable road map for creating breakthroughs.

Dr Abhay Jere, *Chief Innovation Officer, Innovation Cell, Ministry of Human Resource Development, Government of India*

As a Venture Capitalist, I have only one sentence to define the book: *must read for entrepreneurs to avoid costly mistakes.* The most liked chapter for me was 'A Cheat Sheet to New Product Creation' as it provides a complete framework with ample examples. Kaustubh understands and addresses typical challenges an entrepreneur faces in their journey to success with practical examples.

Sanjay Mehta, *Founder and Partner 100X.VC, Mehta Ventures Family Office*

There are very few experts who are able to demystify innovation and Dr Kaustubh Dhargalkar is the foremost among them. Innovation is what gives business ventures the growth that they desperately seek and in Kaustubh's book—*It's Logical: Innovating Profitable Business Models*—they will find all the answers they are seeking. The style of the book is very conversational and simple, shorn of any jargon making the topic look so simple that you will end up asking: how come I did not think about all this before? But then THAT is the secret of a consummate practitioner of this craft like Kaustubh. There are examples given from real-life situations which any entrepreneur can easily identify with, followed up with the logical reasoning and process that has enabled the innovation to come to life—the logic being detailed can be easily applied by entrepreneurs to their businesses to get them the results. While this book would be useful for ALL enterprises, it should be made mandatory reading for all start-ups so that they do not get bogged down by complex moves to gain product superiority. Because, as this book teaches us, anybody can be innovative if they follow the logic!

There are very few experts who are able to demystify innovation and Dr Dhargalkar is the foremost amongst them. I compliment him on his monumental contribution.

Dinkar Suri, *Co-Chair: TiE Academy; CEO and Unconsultant, Retail Market Movers*

With the convergence of an enviable demographic dividend, fast growing economy and rapidly advancing affordable new technologies, the time is ripe for Indian talent to seize the growing opportunities in innovation and entrepreneurship to address various challenges of India and the world. Innovation successes are based not just on the technologies being leveraged but also on a host of other factors such as unique differentiators in the solutions being offered, business models being adopted, networks of relationships developed, financial strategies and having a clear road map to sustainable, profitable growth and expansion of the start-ups or ventures being created.

Dr Kaustubh's book is a timely intervention to all the budding innovators and entrepreneurs be it from the MSME, corporates or universities that provides valuable insights and some thought-provoking stimulation into developing such a clear but simple road map for themselves, both at a high level and breaking it down into smaller components. Breakthrough sustainable and profitable success of any venture is possible only when you also dive into the myriad details that need to be addressed. The book helps the entrepreneur understand, deliberate and creatively adopt models that would be most appropriate for their innovation or business in a lucid manner.

R. Ramanan, *Mission Director, Atal Innovation Mission; Additional Secretary, NITI Aayog*

This book sits at the intersection of management, design and innovation, and merges the boundary between user-centred design and user-centred business innovation. The book is an excellent primer on user-centred business innovation and *strongly advocates 'user first and technology later' approach* throughout the book which is a very welcome move in a tech-dominated world and also debunks the myth that great innovation necessarily has to come from high technology.

The book is written in a very lucid and storytelling format which makes it an interesting read. Dr Kaustubh has done a great job of explaining the underlying technical concepts in a simple language which makes it easy to digest for practitioners.

Another strength of the book is its emphasis on a systemic perspective of looking at the situation considering needs of multiple stakeholders involved in the situation. This is a great addition to the innovation methodology since most of the innovation methods focus on solving problem for a specific user and may not take into consideration the holistic situation with multiple stakeholders leading to the poor adoption of the solution. This is in accordance with a current trend in design field to unite systems thinking methodologies with design methodologies.

The author does not restrict himself only to what's happening in the industry but also goes deeper in reflecting about the Indian education system and how it's killing innovative minds and nurturing a lack of empathy, at an early age, which is an eye-opener for educators.

Overall, this book is an excellent reference not just for innovation practitioners but anyone who needs to understand the value of being user centric in today's hyper competitive business environment.

Shrikant Ekbote, *VP, Design Principal, Barclays Technology Centre India; Research Scholar, Department of Design, IIT Guwahati*

iT'S
LOGICAL

IT'S LOGICAL

Innovating Profitable Business Models

KAUSTUBH DHARGALKAR

Los Angeles | London | New Delhi
Singapore | Washington DC | Melbourne

First published in 2020 by

SAGE Publications India Pvt. Ltd
B1/I-1 Mohan Cooperative Industrial Area
Mathura Road, New Delhi 110 044, India
www.sagepub.in

SAGE Publications Inc
2455 Teller Road
Thousand Oaks, California 91320, USA

SAGE Publications Ltd
1 Oliver's Yard, 55 City Road
London EC1Y 1SP, United Kingdom

SAGE Publications Asia-Pacific Pte Ltd
18 Cross Street #10-10/11/12
China Square Central
Singapore 048423

Published by Vivek Mehra for SAGE Publications India Pvt. Ltd. Typeset in 10.5/13.5 pt Bembo by Fidus Design Pvt. Ltd, Chandigarh.

Library of Congress Control Number: 2020936057

ISBN: 978-93-5388-401-7 (PB)

SAGE Team: Manisha Mathews, Abhilash Dixit, Ankit Verma and Kanika Mathur
Illustrations By: Unmesh Nayak and Namrata Bhagat

To my Param Guru, Swami Satyananda Saraswati,
whose inspirational wisdom I experience every day,
despite his physical non-presence.
And
To my wife, Megha, who has stood solidly by me,
despite my flights of fancy and seemingly whimsical
career shifts.

Thank you for choosing a SAGE product!
If you have any comment, observation or feedback,
I would like to personally hear from you.

Please write to me at **contactceo@sagepub.in**

Vivek Mehra, Managing Director and CEO, SAGE India.

Bulk Sales

SAGE India offers special discounts
for purchase of books in bulk.
We also make available special imprints
and excerpts from our books on demand.

For orders and enquiries, write to us at

Marketing Department
SAGE Publications India Pvt Ltd
B1/I-1, Mohan Cooperative Industrial Area
Mathura Road, Post Bag 7
New Delhi 110044, India

E-mail us at **marketing@sagepub.in**

Subscribe to our mailing list
Write to **marketing@sagepub.in**

This book is also available as an e-book.

Contents

Foreword

Having founded the Industrial Design Centre at IIT Bombay 50 years ago, I have always voiced the need to cultivate an innovative culture within every organization. After my diploma in industrial design from Germany, I worked for Siemens and Telefunken in their research and development units and visited a number of industries in Europe. Their deep commitment to a culture of innovation was strikingly visible.

Groups worked with passion and seriousness to evolve new products and systems. Thirty years ago, I witnessed the pioneering efforts of Philips in developing voice recognition technology at Antwerp in the Netherlands. This technology has only recently become a reality. Seeing the dedication and the time required to go from an innovation to a product left a lasting impression on me. It takes great effort and a long time to develop an innovative culture. Innovation, as is often said, does not fall from the heavens. It takes vision and a strong commitment to the objective. Innovation is hard work!

In contrast to an enduring culture that encourages innovation, I have some reservations about the 'fashion' that innovation centres have become. One cannot innovate in the absence of an ecosystem that drives innovation.

Dr Dhargalkar has vast experience in the space of strategic innovation consulting and design thinking training with conglomerates such as Daimler, Citibank, Mahindra Group, Capgemini, HP, L&T, CEAT tyres, Eaton, TVS Group and so on. He specializes in helping organizations enhance their innovation quotient and has convinced many decision-makers to alter the methods they use to arrive at innovations. His passion, though, lies in being with young minds. He is a highly sought-after professor of design thinking, innovation management and entrepreneurship at various campuses in the country. Notable among these are IIT Bombay, ICT Mumbai (formerly known as University Department of Chemical Technology [UDCT]), IIM Sirmaur, WeSchool, Narsee Monjee Institute of Management Studies (NMIMS), IIT Mandi, etc. Students, across these campuses, would give a limb to attend his courses.

In his avatar as an entrepreneur, his manufacturing unit that designed complex special purpose machines (SPMs) was recognized as a 'mini Japanese factory' by Professor Sasaki, a quality expert from Hamamatsu University and a consultant to many Japanese conglomerates. Considering the fastidiousness of the Japanese towards quality, this is indeed a strong compliment.

This book, supported by deep research and many case studies, shows that it is possible to come up with an innovative business model that does not stick to conventional paradigms. Creating a good business model is like playing cricket—searching for gaps, angling the bat and caressing the ball in the desired direction. It requires a creative yet trained mind. This book tells you exactly how to spot those gaps in the field and train your creative muscle.

As a designer, I know the importance of empathy in creating a user-friendly product. The human being always comes first in any design process. To study the person (the consumer) and to identify all the 'pain points' is as complex as modern medical practice. Dr Dhargalkar's lucid explanation of 'empathy tools' will certainly make you creatively strong and at ease with complex challenges in business.

Over the last two decades, a lot has been said and written about design thinking. Dr Dhargalkar goes beyond the jargon and captures the essence of design thinking in a practical and actionable manner.

Gautam Sarabhai, the renowned industrialist, once explained the importance of context in any creative solution. He said that if you are asked to design a chair, you would obviously think of a seat with four legs, a hand and a back rest. But if you are asked to design something to sit on, then many other possibilities open up. Dr Dhargalkar suggests multiple ways to find a context that open up the possibility of innovation.

I believe that Dr Dhargalkar's discussion on the methods of innovation will be highly useful to corporate managers as well as entrepreneurs.

—Professor Sudhakar Nadkarni
Founder, Industrial Design Centre at IIT Bombay;
Founder, Department of Design at IIT Guwahati;
Widely considered as the 'father' of design education in India

Preface

What's this book about? Most of us think that innovation and creativity lie within the purview of genius. Through this book, I have attempted to debunk that myth and prove that with a sensible head on one's shoulders and relentless focus on the user, 'anyone' can become innovative. All of us are blessed with abundant grey matter that we fail to exploit. This book attempts to provide a pathway to exploit that innate potential within.

The book is a compilation of cases/examples from the entrepreneurial and consulting experience of the protagonist, DK. DK is a unique individual who explores and interprets the world around him through his own lenses. I often tell him that his perspectives to problem-solving are out of the ordinary. Every time that happens, he sits me down and tells me a story from his entrepreneurial and consulting experience wherein he helped the client company come up with an innovative solution. The ideas just blow me away. And then DK in his own inimitable style explains the methodology he employed to help conceptualize the idea and proves to me that it was logic, rather than magic, that made the innovation happen. Believe me, every single time this has happened, I have come out of the room with a reinforced feeling, 'Yes, anybody can be innovative and that innovation and creativity are not the preserve of only the genii.'

The stories in this book are real-life stories of what happened in some situations, while in some others the client company did not have the risk appetite for disruption and therefore didn't go with the solution provided. Some are futuristic 'use cases' through a crystal ball. Be that as it may, each example has some fantastic learning points, which I am certain if utilized in your respective quests for innovation will yield successful results.

Read on to understand DK's approach to innovation. The names of the companies involved have been changed (except where mentioned explicitly), for maintaining confidentiality.

Acknowledgements

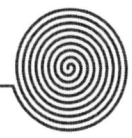

I would like to acknowledge the contributions of my many students who participated enthusiastically in my projects and added a lot of meat to the findings. Some of them who stand out for their enthusiasm are Vijay Manglur, Aditi Nair, Mahek Ganeriwal, Vartika Sethi, Karthik Kumar, Maharshi Sharma, Anupam Mawandia, Sweety Jain, Kasturi Shinde, Yoshita Arora, Meet Ganatra, Tanvi Raorane, Priyal Kumar, Zoya Versey and Anirudh Naik.

My heartfelt gratitude to Professor Dr Uday Salunkhe, the group director of Welingkar Institute of Management Development and Research. As a professor at his institute, he let me experiment with my teaching pedagogy, whereby I could get 'live' corporate challenges into the classroom.

When I read *Blue Ocean Strategy* by W. Chan Kim and Renée Mauborgne, the research bug bit me. Their ability to templatize concepts and make them easily applicable for the common man impressed me a lot.

Eliyahu M. Goldratt, with his classic *The Goal*, made me realize the power of simplifying complex concepts into an engaging storyline with which the reader can easily relate.

My writing style has been greatly influenced by these two books and their authors.

SECTION 1

Innovation Beyond the Esoteric

Chapter 1

Looking Beyond Product Innovation

Can the selling price be below the cost of material?

Let us begin with a small exercise. Tell me what comes to your mind when I say, 'Close your eyes and conjure up images of some cool, innovative stuff, take a minute and list out all those things that come to your mind.'

I do this exercise every time I begin a module on 'innovation'. The answers that I get, about 99 per cent of the time, range from 'an iPhone, Tesla cars, Google glasses to artificial intelligence (AI), virtual reality (VR), augmented reality (AR), machine learning (ML), Space Tech, etc.'

Do you see a common thread in those responses? All the things mentioned, fall into two categories, namely,

1. Hi-end technologies and
2. Physical products

That raises an obvious question in my mind, 'Why are we programmed to associate hi-end technologies and physical products only with innovation?'

'Is innovation restricted to only these categories?'

Let us broaden our understanding of innovation.

Without getting into an intellectual discussion, filled with jargon, let me narrate an experience from DK's entrepreneurial innings.

From 1990 to 2005, DK ran his own manufacturing companies, they were into productivity-enhancement equipment such as automatic

Figure 1.1. Rivets Holding a Fan Blade

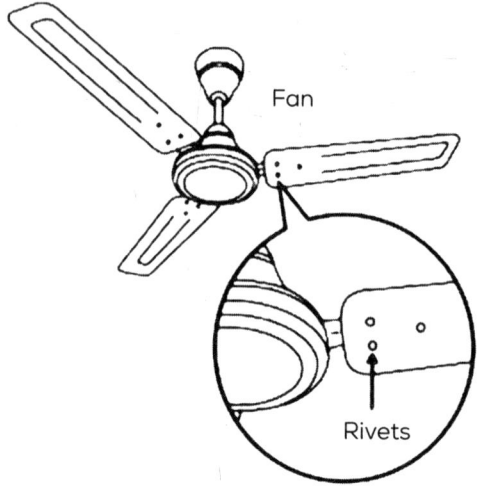

indexing tables, automated conveyor belts, pick and place units, miniature robotics, custom-built machines, etc.

One of their products was something called an automatic riveting machine (ARM). Look at a ceiling fan (Figure 1.1), it generally has three blades fixed onto a motor body with three rivets each.

About 30 years back, fan manufacturers would perform this operation (fixing the fan blade onto the motor body) manually. How? One worker would place the motor body into a fixture, another would place the fan blade and hold it in place, a third would insert the rivets through the holes in the fan blade and the motor body and flatten the rivets with a few hefty blows of a hammer. So basically, three workers would be required to perform the operation.

DK's ARM would enable the same operation with only one worker. A single worker would place the motor body and the fan blade into a fixture under the ARM. At the press of pedal, the ARM would insert the rivet and perform the riveting operation, all in one stroke. The productivity of the assembly line would rise multifold—thrice in terms of manpower and four times in terms of time consumed. The ARM was a fast-moving product for DK.

Figure 1.2. Bakelite Handle Riveted to a Frying Pan

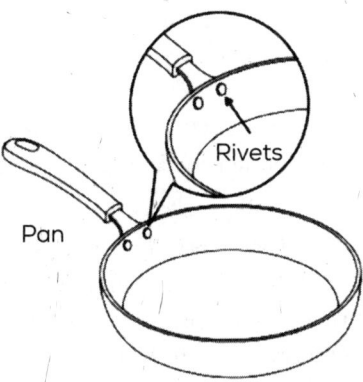

Another major customer segment for the ARMs was cooking utensil manufacturers. A frying pan has a bakelite handle that is riveted onto the main body (Figure 1.2). Some cooking vessels too have handles that are riveted onto them. Hence, the ARMs used to be in great demand in that industry, enhancing the productivity of the assembly lines of utensil manufacturers, many times over.

This incident is about one such customer of DK (you guessed it right!), a cooking utensil manufacturer.

This manufacturer was a large family managed business (FMB), based out of Mumbai. Back in 1998 (when this incident dates back to), they had an annual turnover of ₹290 crores. If translated to today's value, considering inflation over the last 20 years, it would be in the range of ₹2,000–2,200 crores (fairly large for an FMB operating in a largely unorganized domain).

These folks were DK's regular customers since 1990. DK had noticed a peculiar trend in their business. They would sporadically buy an ARM here and there during the year, but once a year they would pick up five to six ARMs in one go. DK had observed this peculiar pattern over the previous seven to eight years and it always intrigued him. Actually, the purchase pattern matched their business cycle. They had a loyal customer from the Middle East. He would pick up a large quantity of their frying pans in one go every year. The logic of his business cycle was that he would sell the frying pans in large numbers, during the holy month of Ramadan, in the Middle East (festive season sales). This Middle Eastern client was a large importer from Dubai, with a well-spread distribution network spanning most of the Gulf countries. As of 1998, this importer would buy frying pans worth around ₹55 crores from the Mumbai manufacturer. Naturally, he was a prized customer (accounting for approximately 20 per cent of an annual turnover of ₹290 crores).

It was the beginning of May 1998. That year, Ramadan was due to commence on December 8th (since Islam follows the lunar calendar, the dates for Ramadan vary every year). Hence, like every year, around six to seven months prior to Ramadan, DK was waiting for a bulk order for his ARMs from the Mumbai manufacturer. On a hot, sultry day in May, he visited them hoping that they would have a purchase order (PO) ready. Due to their decade-old business dealings, DK had a very cordial relationship with the promoters as well as the senior management.

DK was chatting up with the head of production, Mr Singh, sitting in the latter's cabin. About three to four minutes into the conversation, the intercom on Singh's table rang. He picked it up and within the first thirty seconds, DK could sense that something was wrong. Singh's jovial demeanour had changed, his eyebrows were furrowing, pupils dilating, his grip around the receiver had tightened and he was listening intently. DK barely heard anything other than an occasional 'Ohh!', 'How's that possible?' or a 'Yes Sir', accompanied by a blank stare into nowhere. After a couple of minutes, while placing the receiver down onto the cradle, he looked up and blurted, 'There's something extremely urgent that has come up. This was my Managing Director (MD) on the call and I have to rush to his office.... You will have to wait for fifteen minutes.' And he hurried out. The MD's cabin was right next to his and there was a door through the separating wall. DK waited, wondering what had happened. He must have been in there for around half an hour. In those thirty minutes, Singh came in through that door a few times, frantically sifting through papers on his table, sometimes accessing documents from the drawers, picking some and rushing back to the cabin next door. Every time he came through that door, DK could sense something was grossly wrong. In that air-conditioned cabin, sweat was trickling down Singh's brow. The normally confident Singh had his shoulders hunched. On his fourth dash back into his cabin, he looked at DK and said unapologetically, 'Sorry DK, this is not going to end soon, it is too critical. Please come after a couple of weeks.' And he vanished into his MD's office. Trying hard to guess what the situation might be, DK walked out.

A fortnight went by without any contact. DK waited for another ten days. Honestly, his concern was that he hadn't received the bulk purchase order for the ARMs, seven months prior to Ramadan 1999 (six to seven months in advance was the norm). So one fine day, towards the end of May, DK visited their office and walked into Singh's cabin (DK's relationship was informal enough to let him walk in without an appointment). After the initial icebreaker, DK came to the point and asked Singh, 'I presume our PO would be ready? Can I collect it today?'

Singh looked at him in the eye and responded, 'This year we are not buying any of your ARMs.' DK was taken aback and croaked, 'Why?'

Singh: 'We have lost that major order from the Gulf buyer.'

DK: 'What?'

Singh: 'That's what we discovered during your last visit here. Remember the phone call when you were sitting here....'

DK was too shocked to respond, but still managed to ask, 'How?'

Singh continued, 'We have lost that order to a manufacturer from Delhi.'

'But how can a loyal customer just walk away like that?', DK asked.

Singh: 'This Delhi guy has quoted a price which is impossible for us to match. Over the last few weeks, we have tried everything. The math just doesn't add up for us.'

DK: 'Are the Delhi chap's frying pans any good? Are they anywhere comparable to what you guys manufacture?'

Singh: 'We have picked up around 130 frying pans of this Delhi guy, from retail stores all over India and have checked them for quality.

We have conducted all kinds of tests (destructive/non-destructive) possible for mechanical strength, chemical composition, size, material thickness, depth of the anodized coating … you name it … we have tested it. I must say that they are not second to us.' Very grudgingly, Singh added, 'In fact, on three parameters, they are better than us.'

DK's lower jaw dropped as he heard the last sentence.

DK: 'Are they using some recycled aluminium (the main ingredient of a frying pan)?'

Singh: 'I told you we performed specific tests to determine the chemical composition of the aluminium that they use. It's absolutely top-drawer quality.'

DK: 'Maybe the other components, the rivets, the Bakelite handles, etc. are substandard?'

Singh (somewhat irritated): 'No … if you are so curious to know, let me share the entire analysis with you, with an example of one of the frying pan specifications that we export. Our maximum retail price (MRP) in India is ₹355. Our price to the Gulf importer, for the same frying pan, is ₹195 (a clean 45% bulk discount considering the volume). This Delhi guy has quoted ₹128 for exactly the same frying pan. Now take a paper and pen and write down the numbers that I tell you.'

DK borrowed a sheet of paper from Singh's table.

Singh: 'The frying pan needs 900 gm of aluminium. We buy it at ₹120 a kg. How much would it be for 900 gm?' (mocking DK).

DK: '108.'

Singh: 'Good, write down all the material costs, Bakelite handle ₹3.30, stainless steel rivets ₹1.25, anodized coating ₹5.17....' he went on narrating the costs, right up to that of the paper carton.

Singh: 'Now, add it up.'

DK (running the pen up and down the column): '₹137.27'

Singh, then waited, looking at DK, to check whether he had realized the irony of it all.

Just to reconfirm his addition, DK ran through it again and said, 'Singh, this is impossible. Did you give me the right numbers? ... your cost of material is more than the Delhi chap's selling price.... Are you sure about the costs that you told me?'

Singh (emphatically): 'To the last penny.'

DK (shaking his head): 'I'm sure, they must be sourcing substandard material at very low prices.'

Singh: 'Remember all the testing done by us on their frying pans? We had picked up their products from retailers all across India.' In a hushed tone, he added, 'If this is the quality of their products in India ... the quality of their export items must actually be even better.'

Singh continued, 'In the last three weeks, we have found everything that is to know about this guy. He sources his aluminium (which comprises almost 80% of the material cost) from HINDALCO (Hindustan Aluminium Company, an Aditya Birla group company). We too, source our aluminium from them. We have been their customers for the last twenty years. We have been able to find the price at which they sell it to the Delhi guy ... we got this information due to our contacts in the system, (generally, it's confidential information). And to our surprise, HINDALCO sells the same grade of aluminium (as what we buy from them) at a three percent higher price to the Delhi guy than what they sell it to us at, that is, what we pay ₹120 a kg for, the Delhi chap pays ₹123.60.'

DK: 'Why the difference?'

Singh: 'Because, we buy about 20 times more aluminium from HINDALCO than this Delhi manufacturer ... and HINDALCO acknowledges that with a better price.... So we have an advantage over him in terms of raw material. The same advantage applies to other components too. We have found his other costs too.' 'His cost of material adds up to ₹146.52, against ours at ₹137.27, got it?'

For DK, all this was unbelievable, but Singh's detailed explanation seemed logical.

Summarizing it all up, DK said, 'That means his selling price is less than his cost of material', trying to grasp the accounting significance of that statement.

Getting more analytical, DK said, 'This Delhi smarty must be having some super-efficient manufacturing processes to cut down his processing costs....'

Singh interrupted, looked disdainfully at DK and asked, in a measured tone (trying not to let his emotion get the better of him), 'Haven't you ever seen a Profit & Loss account?'

DK was perplexed. Singh continued, 'Where do the processing costs get reflected? After the material costs, right?'

DK nodded.

He went on, 'Then if you include his processing costs, his cost of manufacturing would be even higher, that is, higher than ₹146.52, right? My guess ... it would go up to ₹169. I have spent enough years in this industry to guess that with ± 2 per cent accuracy. Which means, he is incurring a huge loss on the entire shipment. Remember, he is selling at ₹128.'

DK interjected, 'He is probably entering the market at a loss, with the sole purpose of grabbing the customer from you, holding the pricing for the next 2–3 years and then raise his prices big time to recover his losses.' DK felt as though he had aced an organic chemistry quiz.

Singh replied, 'For this to happen, this Delhi guy has to be sitting on piles of cash reserves, such that he can bear losses for the first few years.' Singh went on, 'Actually, I missed mentioning this to you earlier. In order to get to know our competitor well, we have employed two detective agencies to find out everything about this company, its promoters, in fact everything that is there to know about these guys. This is a start-up venture barely a year-old, run by a sole proprietor, with absolutely no back up. So he has no cash reserves to sustain any kind of losses. This is his first big order! Let me share a secret with you. We even have his horoscope!'

Singh took out two envelopes from his drawer and placed them on the table, in front of DK. DK looked at them, trying to make sense of all that Singh was saying. Singh had a wry smile that showed through his beard, 'These came from our detectives and they match! We know everything about this man. He comes from a middle-class family. Father is a retired bank clerk; mom was a junior accountant in a local hardware store. He has no access to fancy funds. Neither is he married into a rich family, nor does his wife belong to a politician's family. You understand what I mean by that? There's no one bankrolling cash to him. He just doesn't have the means to survive the loss?'

So now, my readers, can you figure out what was happening here? Take a break and list your guesses about how this Delhi manufacturer managed this coup d'état.

UNFOLDING THE MYSTERY

Back in the 1990s, India was a foreign exchange starved economy, that is, there would barely be Forex reserves to cover a couple of months of the import bill for crude oil. Hence, Indian exporters would be heavily incentivized through various schemes, since exporters bring the much-needed dollars into the country. One such scheme was referred to as Duty Drawback policy. As per the policy (back in 1999), an Indian exporter would be entitled to an import license in the ratio of 1:1, that is, if you exported goods worth ₹X from India, you would automatically be entitled to an import license of ₹X.

Now, understand how the Delhi manufacturer was using this Duty Drawback policy.

As mentioned earlier, the Mumbai manufacturer's export shipment would be worth about ₹55 crores. An exactly identical shipment was being exported by the Delhi manufacturer at approximately ₹36 crores.

$$
\left\{
\begin{array}{c}
\text{Export price of the Delhi manufacturer/Export price} \\
\text{of the Mumbai manufacturer} = 128/195 = 0.656 \\
0.656 \times ₹55 \text{ crores} = ₹36.1 \text{ crores}
\end{array}
\right\}
$$

Against an export shipment of ₹36 crores, the Delhi manufacturer was getting an import license of an equivalent amount (₹36 crores).

Very smartly, on that import license, he was importing such items that could fetch around 300 per cent markup in the Indian market, that is, the goods he imported at the rate of ₹36 crores, he could sell at around ₹105 crores in the Indian market.

Now, understand the math carefully.

How much was the loss that the Delhi manufacturer was incurring on his export shipment?

$$₹55 \text{ crores} – ₹36 \text{ crores} = ₹19 \text{ crores}$$

How much profit was he earning on his import shipment?

$$₹105 \text{ crores} – ₹36 \text{ crores} = ₹69 \text{ crores}$$

So overall, he was making a surplus of

$$₹69 \text{ crores} – ₹19 \text{ crores} = ₹50 \text{ crores}$$

Hence, the apparently loss-making business of exporting frying pans at a price well below his cost of material, was actually a profit-making transaction for the Delhi manufacturer.

Now, my questions to you, all my readers:

1. Was there any hi-end technology involved?
2. Was there any product innovation introduced by the Delhi manufacturer?

Neither of the above.

But the Delhi manufacturer managed to beat a much larger and well-entrenched incumbent. In fact, the Mumbai-based company never recovered from this shock.... They wound up operations and shut down about eleven months later. They could not recover from a 20 per cent hit to their revenues.

Now, this raises a question:

Why did the Mumbai manufacturer not follow the Delhi manufacturer in utilizing the Duty Drawback policy?

Well, that's easier said than done. Due to the sudden hole of 20 per cent in their revenue, their cash flows suffered badly. Once cash flows went for a toss:

- They could not pay their vendors on time and as a result, their purchase schedules suffered.

- They could not pay their workers on time. The workers went on a 'go-slow' agitation. A section of them, affiliated to a particularly strident union, went on strike. This led to the company being unable to fulfil customer orders.

- Delayed deliveries to customers were enough to spread all kinds of rumours in the market. When customers (even long-standing ones) heard about the striking workers and the 'go-slow' agitation, they began to look for other manufacturers.

All in all, it proved to be a downward spiral, more like a black hole, from which there was no return.

Another important question might have come to your mind:

Why hadn't the Mumbai manufacturer utilized the import licenses effectively against their earlier shipments (after all, they were exporting to the Gulf for many years prior to this incident)?

Well, they would definitely use those import licenses. But they would buy fancy machinery and equipment from Germany, Japan and Taiwan to upgrade their assembly lines. They never looked at the import licenses as creatively as the Delhi manufacturer did. In fact, many a time, their import licenses would lapse (due to disuse within a particular financial year).

The Mumbai manufacturer looked at itself as a frying pan manufacturer only, while the Delhi manufacturer, probably, looked at his business as a means to manage and multiply his funds.... Frying pan manufacturing, for him, was just a means to manage and multiply his funds.

This is a classic case of Business Model Innovation, going beyond product and technological innovation. More about Business Model Innovation in the next chapter.

IMPRESSIVE IMPRESSIONS

When you think of innovation, think beyond just the product and technology. Pay close attention to your business model.

1. 'Try not to let one customer over-populate your order book': The Gulf-based importer comprised around 20 per cent of the Mumbai manufacturer's order book. If it was a lesser component, probably, the Mumbai folks might have been able come out of the shock, albeit with a little damage, but more importantly, with a valuable lesson learnt.

2. 'Keep looking for alternate revenue streams': The Delhi manufacturer was always on the lookout for direct/indirect opportunities.

3. 'Scan the ecosystem like a hawk ... with no let-up': Constantly, keep scanning the entire value chain in the ecosystem. You never know where the next opportunity could come from.

4. 'A Business Model is perpetually in a WIP (Work in Progress) mode': Consequently, with the changing ecosystem, keep re-examining your business model and tweak it whenever necessary.

Business Model Innovation vs Product or Technology Innovation

Coming up with a new product or new technology is far more difficult than relooking at the business model. The journey of product or technology innovations is an arduous one, involving time, effort and deep domain knowledge. I am not saying that these attributes are not necessary for bringing about business model innovation. I am only evaluating the two on a comparative scale and business model innovation appears the easier of the two.

Moreover, from a manager's perspective, business model innovation seems easier because most of the parameters required to make that happen are more or less under her/his control and are more easily tweakable (if such a word exists).

I reiterate, I am not, for a moment, saying that business model innovation is superior to either product or technological innovation, I am just saying that it is the easier of the two for a business executive.

Chapter 2

Thou Shall Create Win-Win Situations

What does it take to succeed in business?

A great product? A great service? An untapped, niche market? If you have any of these, there's a high likelihood of business success, right?

What if you don't have any of these? Is your business doomed to fail? Conventional logic says, yes? However, I believe that's not necessarily true. If you have an ordinary product/service offering, you can still create a successful business. You could create unique ways of reaching out to your target group, you could figure out new and unique collaborative platforms which can be monetized. One can create value for the consumer by creating value for everyone in the ecosystem. For someone to benefit, another doesn't have to lose. Learn to create win-win situations in business. To reinforce this point, I am going to cite some examples from the recent past (the last decade) of how some companies built their businesses by creating win-win situations.

MANTRAS FOR CREATING WIN-WIN SITUATIONS IN BUSINESS

Yes, there are. I am going to share some findings from my research spanning the last few years.

About eight years ago, I began to look for businesses (small and large) which **did not have any breakthrough technologies or products**, yet commanded good customer traction. As I came across more and more such businesses, I started seeing some typical traits that these businesses displayed. The quest spanned 90 companies functioning across all continents. The focus, as mentioned earlier, was not on companies with blockbuster technologies or products, but on companies that went around doing their business differently, that is, companies offering regular products or services but doing so in unique ways. The companies analysed were from multiple sectors ranging from **retail, hospitality, FMCG, mobility, education, fashion, recruiting, entertainment** to **NGOs**.

I will share some traits that I picked up from these business models. Let me add a disclaimer here. The founders of these companies may not have started with these traits in mind. They may have had different intentions for starting their ventures. However, my analysis tells me that these are the basic traits or building blocks which define the entire business model. According to me, these building blocks are the learning points from this chapter and are replicable in any domain. So dear readers, please look at these from the angle of how you could adopt them in your business domains.

Here's the first one.

Double Whammy

Milking both ends of the value chain, that is, making money from the consumers as well as the backend service vendors.

Hair styling salons, by Jawed Habib Hair & Beauty Ltd, with its brand of Hair Xpreso outlets, offer designer haircuts to the Indian youth at an extremely affordable price (beginning as low as ₹149). In fact, when they started operations a decade back, it was as low as ₹99.

Most stylists employed at these outlets are students at Jawed Habib's Hair Academy. The company charges these trainees a regular training fee and these trainees, in turn, get to hone their newly acquired skills on paying customers. In effect, the company makes money from consumers as well as the employees/suppliers (in this case the trainees), that is, from both ends of the value chain. Hair Xpreso is able to keep the prices low because of the lower operating costs, creating a win-win situation for all involved. Low prices for the consumer and on-the-job experience for the trainees to hone their skills.

Duolingo, is a company that gamifies learning foreign languages. It follows a freemium model for the language learning material that it creates. On closer study, we realized that Duolingo is actually a company that offers 'translation services'. The way it has structured its organization is very interesting. The documents that it receives for translation are broken down into small paragraphs/sentences/words/ etc. The contents are then animated to create small language learning tutorials, that are fun to use. Duolingo, then uploads these animations on Google Play and the Apple App Store, from where netizens can download and use them to learn the language. Imagine hundreds of thousands of individuals attempting the translations. Duolingo, at the backend captures all these attempts, chooses the best translations from across the games created from the original document, stitches them together and voila ... the entire document is ready, translated, not just at zero cost, but, with its freemium model, Duolingo makes money from 'paying' users too. It not only makes money from fees charged for translating the document but also from the users who pay to learn a foreign language. This is another classical example of Double Whammy and my favourite one. Once again, a win-win situation ... low learning cost for the language learning aspirant and low translation cost for the translation-seeking customer.

'Where can one use this trait to build a unique business model?'

This trait, double whammy, can be used in sectors where you are running a business and you find that there is an opportunity of training people in sufficiently large numbers. You can build a business training those folks as well as using them as service providers. Look how a medical college runs: it has a hospital attached to it. A lot of the junior resident doctors at the hospital are interns from their own medical college, that is, paying students and paying patients. Can you spot more opportunities for the medical college to grow?

As of now, most of these colleges don't run training schools for nurses. An ideal ratio for doctors to nurses in India is 1:3. Currently, according to the National Development Council India has only 1.6 nurses per doctor. That translates to a shortfall of six million nurses.[1] Imagine the untapped opportunity there. These numbers are restricted only to nurses. If you consider the numbers for other healthcare staff, that would be a mind-boggling opportunity.

Monetizing a Third Party's NVA

Identify someone else's non-value adding asset (NVA) and helping them monetizing it.

Cashurdrive Marketing Pvt Ltd is a creative media company, based out of New Delhi that offers innovative media solutions. Vehicle 'wraps' is one such solution that they offer to advertisers. Most of us drive our cars for about 40 to 50 kilometres everyday around the city. The outer shell of our car is visible to everyone, everywhere we go and hence, it makes for great advertising space. They register car owners who are willing to let the outer shell of their car be used for putting up advertisements of various companies. The registered car owners get a monthly/quarterly/annual fee in return which subsidizes their loan EMI.

'What has this company done here?' Simply put, they identified someone's NVA asset (the outer shell of one's car) which is a great advertising space $24 \times 7 \times 365$ and created a revenue stream for themselves as well as the car owner.

That's a great win-win for both!

Have you heard of 'Ringback Tone Advertising'?

Mobile service providers across the world, let you subscribe to their 'caller tune' facility and charge you a micro amount for that, by letting you choose/customize your ringtone. What's happening here? Whenever someone calls you, instead of the usual tring ... tring ... they would hear, till you accept the call, the caller tune that you have

---

[1] https://economictimes.indiatimes.com/industry/healthcare/biotech/healthcare/india-facing-shortage-of-600000-doctors-2-million-nurses-study/articleshow/68875822.cms

chosen. The time that you hold for, before getting connected, is idle time for you, right? In other words, it is an NVA for you. Can it be monetized? Yes, of course.

Who makes money here? The appropriate rights of the song/tune are bought by the mobile service providers (MSPs), that is, the MSP pays the artist. Sometimes this works the other way around too, if it's a new artist, the artist is the one who pays the MSP, to popularize his song/tune. The MSP makes money by making the subscriber pay for setting the tune on her/his phone number. The artist's benefit is that her/his song/tune gets heard by all those who call you. It helps popularize the artist's creation.

'A win–win situation', for everyone involved:

- The MSP gets the subscription fee that you pay for the caller tune facility
- You have the choice of placing some cool music as your ringtone
- The artist's creation gets popularized

Now, let's drill this down further in DK's style, to make it even more monetizable and valuable for the stakeholders involved.

Imagine a company called Adjinglia (don't google it, it's a fictional one). Currently, its business is playing advertisements of various companies instead of songs or tunes. The subscriber gets some freebies like some reward points/cashback/movie tickets/ etc. This is already being done by many MSPs across the world.

Let us see how Adjinglia can monetize this further by creating more value for the stakeholders involved.

Suppose tomorrow onwards Adjinglia says, 'The more you talk on your mobile phone, the lesser you have to pay!'

Adjinglia introduces a few assorted plans say, a 15-second plan or a 30-second plan or a 45-second plan. You, the customer of any MSP, subscribes to one of these plans for free (no hidden charges). To avail of the service, you would have to download Adjinglia's app onto your mobile phone.

The new idea: Suppose you have subscribed to the 30-second plan, then every time you call a friend, the friend's phone does not ring[2] for 30 seconds (after the connection is complete) and in those 30 seconds, you are made to listen to an advertisement that Adjinglia pushes into the system.

Now, imagine something more interesting. Every time, a friend calls you, your phone does not ring for 30 seconds (after the connection is complete) and for those 30 seconds, your friend has to listen to the advertisement Adjinglia pushes into the system.

The more you call your friends and the more your friends call you, the lesser are your mobile phone charges. Adjinglia's app keeps track of the number of seconds you and your friends have heard the advertisements and credits your account accordingly. All this became possible because you subscribed to Adjinglia's service and became a conduit for the advertisements of various companies. You get paid because you have proved to be a medium for virality. In the digital world, such folks are called 'influencers'. These influencers get paid handsomely. For a lot of them, it is their main or only source of income and it's huge. So why not extend it to the slightly low-tech world of voice telephony?

Everyone wins in this model.

- The consumer, that is you, gets rewarded in the form of lower usage charges (if you are one those *yakety yak* types who constantly chatter on your phone, then you could actually get paid beyond just offsetting your mobile phone charges).

- The advertisers, who get so many more ears to hear out their proposition

- Adjinglia, the aggregator gets paid by the advertisers for increasing their reach.

---

[2] You can disable the 30-second delay any time you want to (e.g., if you want to make an emergency call).

 It's Logical: Innovating Profitable Business Models

Please note how the standard 'caller tune' model has been dissected and more value created for all the stakeholders involved. That's the beauty of business model innovation, it's not difficult to execute, provided you figure how to create, yes, you guessed, 'win-win situations'.

Let us look at a more famous example.

Uber launched its beta version in May 2010, with its operations in the city of San Francisco. Initially, the service was restricted to black luxury cars only.

'Why only luxury cars?' Outside a five-star hotel, one always sees hi-end vehicles with a 'T' symbol. These are basically taxis that the guests can hire. Are these cars owned by the hotel? No, most of these are leased out by fleet rental companies s.a. Hertz, Budget, Orix, etc. Do they have customers all the time? No, they are empty most of the time (an independent study claims that around 35 per cent to 40 per cent of the time they have no customers). Are they happy with this situation? Obviously not. The vehicles in question, usually, are BMWs (5 or 7 series), Mercedes (E-class and above). Any sane business person would want her/his expensive assets utilized to as close to 100 per cent as possible.

The Uber founders, probably, realized this and created the now-famous geo-location platform and approached the fleet rental companies asking them, 'Would you take rides when your cars are idle?'

Would the fleet rental company refuse? Why would they? That offer would enable them to monetize their expensive assets to the maximum possible and that too, without hampering their existing business. They would be paid per kilometre.

For the cab commuter, it's cheaper than hiring that expensive car.

A 'perfect win-win situation' as:

1. The fleet rental company gets business during its idle hours (when its car is actually an NVA).

2. The commuter gets a reasonable price for his commute.

3. Uber gets a commission and creates a transportation business without investing in a single vehicle.

Post the success of this 'monetizing a third party's NVA' model, with the fleet rental companies, Uber quickly sold the idea to individual cab owners. Gradually, people bought cars on their own and logged onto the Uber platform.

Airbnb too have done the same thing. They identified someone else's NVA assets and built an aggregator platform to enable the asset-owners make money and, in the process, have created value for themselves.

Be it Cashurdrive or the fictitious Adjinglia, Uber or Airbnb, 'all of them have created win-win situations for everyone involved....'

1. The asset-owners (a private car owner in case of Cashurdrive, a cabbie in the case of UBER and a homeowner in the case of Airbnb) are forever worried about paying off their EMIs. And all these companies have created an avenue for the asset owners to monetize their assets.

2. Availability has increased for the consumer seeking these services.

3. Consequently, the demand-supply interdependence brings the prices down, benefiting the consumer.

Everybody wins in the process. 'The business model creates value for all the players in the ecosystem.'

Zero Inventory of Your Own

If you can help monetize someone else's NVA, then, as a corollary, you can do business with zero (or almost zero) inventory of your own. In management jargon, such a model would be referred to as an 'asset-light model'. This is pretty self-explanatory, so let us not spend time on it.

Fractional Ownership

Selling an asset to a group of customers.

Netjets is a company which is in the business of selling private aircrafts. Now, who do you think buys aircrafts for private use? Super, super rich folks, right? How many such people exist in the world? Not many. At some point, the market is going to get saturated.

It's not a volume market, so about 20–25 years back, Netjets were wondering, what next? A little bit of research threw up the fact that there was a segment of slightly less rich people, who were equally busy but they didn't have the cash flow to buy an aircraft at one go. Aircrafts don't come cheap. Imagine this hotshot business guy has to be in Germany tomorrow for a client meeting. Without a private aircraft he has to rely on commercial airlines. Commercial airlines have fixed timetables. They are not going to change timings for an individual and when you take a commercial flight you have to check-in 2 hours in advance. It's a lot of time wasted for an extremely busy person. But remember he is not that rich that he can own his own private aircraft. Netjets identified such people as a new segment and started selling aircrafts to these people in groups. Like 5–6 people in that segment buy one aircraft fractionally. Imagine, I'm Netjets and you are a group of six such people. I sell one aircraft to you six as a group. The cost is shared by you all as per each one's capacity, say, one of you pays 10 per cent, the other 15 per cent, the other 18 per cent and so on, totalling to 100 per cent. The flying hours are then shared by your group in the ratio of your investment. That is, the aircraft is owned fractionally by the group.

Is there a problem here? Of course, there is. Suppose two of you (from the same group) want to fly at the same time. Now what?

Netjets hasn't sold only one aircraft to one group. It has sold another 80–100 aircrafts to another 80–100 groups. It's highly unlikely that everybody wants to fly at the same time. If two people from the same group want to fly at the same time, Netjets can offer another aircraft which is idle otherwise. Now, does this create another problem? Of course, it does.

Suppose Netjets has sold one group a Beechcraft and two from that group want to fly at the same time and suppose one of them gets a Beechcraft and other gets a Cessna. Won't the other guy say, 'Hey, I bought a Beechcraft and you are making me fly in a Cessna, what the hell?'

That forces Netjets to have a standardized fleet. Either all Beechcrafts or all Cessnas. This actually makes things simpler for Netjets. They don't have to maintain an inventory of different spare parts for different types of aircrafts and aircraft spares are expensive ... so a standardized fleet makes Netjets a lean organization. Another advantage of standardization is that, Netjets doesn't have to have different pilots for different aircrafts. As per Aviation regulations, a pilot who flies one type of an aircraft cannot be suddenly shifted to fly a different type, she/he has to undergo certain simulation hours in between. So the airline company has to maintain extra pilots for contingencies such as pilots calling in sick, etc. Because Netjets has a standardized fleet, shifting one pilot from an aircraft to another doesn't become a problem as the type of aircraft is the same. Netjets would have had to maintain 15–20 per cent extra pilots if they had not standardized, but with standardization they have to maintain just about the number required and maybe 2–5 per cent extra. That means, a non-standardized fleet would have 20 per cent extra pilots. How much does a pilot cost per year? Probably, 10–25 millions of rupees, considering the cost to the company (CTC: salary, insurance, travel allowances, etc.). Twenty per cent extra pilots on, say, a base of 100 means, a non-standardized fleet is already down by 200–500 millions of rupees on day one, with no revenue. That is why airline companies like Indigo fly only Airbus 320s (not even a variation, say Airbus 300). The same applies to in-flight crew too. Cabin crew cannot be moved from one type of aircraft to another without an intervening training/simulation period.

Plus, when an airline buys only one type of aircraft in bulk, the airline's bargaining power with the manufacturer is much higher. That's the power of standardization; the entire business structure changes.

This approach opened up a completely new segment for Netjets.

Let's explore the Netjets model further. Now each of the fractional owners of the aircraft will have the headache of maintenance of the aircraft, managing the pilots, the crew, etc. So Netjets tells these people, 'You don't worry about anything, we will take care of maintenance, in-flight crew, pilots, on-ground staff, etc., in return for a subscription fee.' So from a pure product company, Netjets transformed itself into a hybrid, product-cum-service company.

The advantages of such a business model are:

1. The customer has to pay a lower upfront cost for owning an asset.

2. The airline company generates a recurring revenue source for the entire lifespan of the product.

3. The operating costs of the airline company dropped drastically, as seen earlier, due to standardization of its fleet.

Do win-win situations get any better?

'When can you use such a business model?'

When you are trying to sell expensive stuff, you can use this fractional ownership kind of a model. Where finding one single buyer, due to high product cost, is tough, you can experiment with this kind of a model.

Let's look at other examples which you might be more familiar with.

Time Share Holidays: Say, Mahindra Holidays, Sterling Resorts, etc. suppose I want to spend some time in Kodaikanal but can't afford a house there. Do I have to buy a house? I can subscribe to Mahindra or Sterling Resorts and spend 6–7 days without owning a property there. It is fractionally owned by members like me from whom they take a one-time fee and an annual subscription fee and the members can use their property at available locations. Isn't that fractional ownership?

If you are in the business of selling high-priced products or services, see, if you can use this kind of a model.

Service First, Business Later

Offer your services first, even before the consumer pays you. Think about making her/him pay later.

Now, this sounds completely crazy. How can you offer services to someone who is not buying your services? That just doesn't make any business sense, right?

Ping An, a Chinese BFSI (banking, financial services, insurance) conglomerate does just that. How can a bank or an insurance company offer services without asking the consumer to pay for it?

Ping An created an online platform called Good Doctor in August 2014. The company's vision for the platform is, 'To provide every family with a family doctor, every person with an e-health profile and everyone with a healthcare management plan'. It began as an online service where anyone would get doctor consultations for free. The point to be noted here was that the users of the Good Doctor platform were not Ping An's customers. In April 2015, the company launched the Ping An Good Doctor app. By providing the healthcare services, the platform generated tremendous traction. By December 2018, the app had 265 million registered users with 54.7 million monthly active users (MAU).[3] All these services are offered free to the registered users.

So is there any business logic to this?

Approximately, 35 per cent of Ping An's new users have come from this platform and now they are 'paying customers'. Now, do you get what I meant by the motto, 'Service First, Business Later'? Ping An now monetizes its user base (265 million as of December 2018) to expand its footprint in the healthcare and wellness space. As of May 2019, it had more than 2,000 healthcare institutions as partners,[4] including physical examination centres, dental clinics, cosmetic surgery units and more than 15,000 pharmacy outlets providing relevant health and wellness services to their users. Can you imagine the magnitude of the business this must be generating? Ping An has used (is using and will use) the Good Doctor platform to expand its footprint in multiple domains, thus creating revenue streams which they would not have imagined back in 2013. In fact, if you examine the platform closely, you will notice that, on the platform, there are multiple competitors of Ping An's core business. So in effect, every

[3] https://www.mobihealthnews.com/news/asia-pacific/ping-good-doctor-expands-finance-through-cooperation-china-everbright-bank
[4] http://www.pahtg.com/en/about-us/company-overview/

time a competitor makes a sale on the Good Doctor platform, Ping An too makes money in the form of a small commission. The data that it collects about the competitors and consumers is a bonus. This data will help Ping An build more revenue streams in the future. One could call this as, 'aggregating competitors on a platform' (more about this in detail in the next paragraph).

Every time, a partner on the Good Doctor app does a transaction, Ping An too makes money. Win-win situations don't get any better.

Every stakeholder in the ecosystem wins in the process:

1. The users get free consultations.

2. Ping An acquires new customers.

3. The partner institutions acquire new customers.

4. These customers are not one-time users. Healthcare needs are a recurring requirement.

Ping An creates a positive affinity with the intended user and then sells them services related to their requirements. A wonderful win-win situation, by providing *service first* and thinking about *business later!*

- As a corollary to 'Service First, Business Later', another interesting trait comes out, which can be referred to as, 'aggregating competitors on a platform': Bringing multiple competitors on a common platform and targeting a particular consumer segment

Back in 2007–2008, there was a service run by two IIT-Delhi students called www.phokatcopy.com that enabled students to get their photocopying done free of cost.

Free of cost?

Yes, absolutely free of cost. Here's how? They tied up with various photocopy vendors. The understanding with these vendors was as follows:

For any student-customer who walked in, for every ₹20 worth of photocopying, the vendor would give a scratch card to the student. The scratch card used to be nicely branded by www.phokatcopy.com (created and printed by the owners of www.phokatcopy.com).

The vendor would charge his normal price for the photocopying (not a penny less).

The scratch card had clear usage instructions. On scratching the card, the user would see a code number. This number had to fed into the relevant window on www.phokatcopy.com An encashable discount coupon would then appear on screen. The user would have to take a printout of this coupon (remember, back then freebies/cashbacks were not sent via WhatsApp/SMS, one had to take a printout and present it at the vendor's to avail the discount) at the vendors' such as Wimpy's, Nirulas, etc., (www.phokatcopy.com had tie-ups with these vendors). Against these coupons, the student would then get an equivalent discount, i.e. if a student had bought photocopies worth say, ₹40, then he would get two scratch cards of ₹20 each and hence two encashable discount coupons worth ₹40. The next time the student went to a Wimpy's or a Nirulas outlet, he could get a discount of ₹40 on his total spend. The amount of discount encashed had a limit per transaction, that is, if a student had discount coupons worth, say ₹100, then he would be able to encash them worth, say ₹60 now and ₹40 on her/his next visit.

This meant that a student's photocopies would actually be rendered free. Think through the entire transaction, there's no hanky-panky. The photocopying is actually free for the student.

'How would www.phokatcopy.com make money?' They would get a commission on every customer that visited a Wimpy's/Nirulas (they added many more to the network later) outlet and encashed the coupon.

'Why would these vendors pass on the commission?' Because they would acquire a possible new customer through the inducement of a discount coupon created by www.phokatcopy.com. Their acquisition cost for a new customer would come down.

'Why would the photocopy vendor bother to keep the scratch cards?' The founders of www.phokatcopy.com were smart not to keep the scratch cards at every photocopy vendor in the same locality. They would keep them only at around 50–60 per cent of the vendors in the vicinity of a college. This meant that students would flock to those vendors who kept the scratch cards, thus increasing the revenue of those vendors who had a tie-up with www.phokatcopy.com.

'The student would be the primary beneficiary.' Do I need to explain how?

Everyone involved with www.phokatcopy.com would win in the process, isn't it?

'When does this kind of a business model make sense?'

Many a time, demand for a product or service is catered to by multiple unconnected business entities spread all over. One can create a platform where the entire demand for a product/service is aggregated and serviced.

'A smarter way of using this approach' might be when you are trying to enter a highly crowded and hence, competitive market, where there already are too many players and capturing market share from each other is extremely difficult. While entering such a market, you could launch a platform that aggregates all your competitors on one platform and help them sell their services/products too. In effect, every time your competitors make a sale on the platform, you make money in the form of a commission on that sale.

Help others to help yourselves! Business is not antipodal to spirituality!

Pay for What You Use

Don't charge a customer a penny more than what she uses (no hidden charges).

Samoa Air, till 2015, would charge a customer by the weight they carried (body weight plus weight of their luggage) and not as per seat. Their online booking page said, 'Give us your weight … within a *kilo* (kg) or two would be fine, then tell us how much baggage you want to take, you can take as many bags as you like but just give us the intended total of your baggage in *kilos* (a *kilo* is 2.2 pounds). We will add all of this together and charge by the *kilo* against the sector fare which is always in our local currency (the Samoan Tala) and that is your total airfare ... simple.' They had a base fare per kg (depending on the route). This base fare would be multiplied by the declared weight to calculate the total fare.

What did they do here? They told us that they would charge us exactly on the basis of how much we use. The airline had a fleet of light aircrafts, which are highly weight sensitive.... The airline promised that a larger person would get more space, a taller person would get more legs pace, but would have to pay more for it. A smaller person would get less space and would have to pay less for it. Sounds logical ... the fuel consumption of the aircraft is directly proportional to the weight it carries. So they charged their customers based on 'how much they used'.

Isn't that a new way to look at airline pricing? Everybody benefits in the process:

- The larger person gets more space (so pays more).
- The smaller person gets less space (so pays less).
- The airline benefits when they can recover the cost per flight, based on how much fuel is consumed during the flight.

'Another way to create win–win situations!'

Imagine, if an automobile manufacturer sold you a vehicle against 20 per cent upfront payment and then charged on the basis of your usage, for example, if you drove on a smooth expressway, you would pay, say, ₹15 per kilometre and if you drove over a rough country road, you would pay, say, ₹20 per kilometre and so on. These numbers would be different for different models. Would you go for such a pricing plan? This is 'pay for what you use', in action. The benefits of the process:

- The consumer has to pay a lower upfront instalment.
- The automobile manufacturer monetizes the entire lifespan of the vehicle.
- Telematics in the car enables the automobile manufacturer to track the driving habits, performance of the vehicle under multiple conditions. This data would be a great source of insights for the R&D folks.

Another form of the 'pay for what you use' model would translate into compliance-based pricing in the insurance industry.

This one is related to one of DK's projects with a Health Insurance company.

Current Scenario

Today, insurance companies charge premium based on the age and health-risk profile of an individual. If two individuals, A and B of the same age, with a similar health-risk profile, buy the same insurance plan. Further, if both A and B were mildly diabetic and coincidentally, had a similar blood sugar reading (at the time of the commencement of a life insurance policy). In today's scenario, both are charged the same premium. However, imagine a scenario wherein, individual A complies better with the treatment drugs and recommended dietary restrictions, individual B does not comply as well. Consequently, A's blood sugar levels are much more in control than B's. Obviously, B is a higher risk for the insurance company, but under the current insurance plan, both keep paying the same insurance premium. Is this a fair model?

Proposed Scenario in Light of the Internet of Things (IOT) Revolution

Now, imagine, if the insurance company had a system of recording both, A's and B's blood sugar levels and other parameters on a regular basis and capture that information on the cloud, they would know the compliance levels of both, A and B and consequently, would be aware of the increased risk levels of individual B. In such a case, ideally, B should be charged a higher premium than what A pays. Today, we have numerous non-invasive devices for checking these health parameters. Such devices could monitor an individual's health parameters such as blood sugar level, etc., and synch them with the insurance company's cloud. The insurance company could keep a track of the compliance and risk levels of its customers and introduce variable premium insurance plans (charging B more than it does A, in the above scenario).

It's a win-win situation: If such a system existed, not only would the risk come down for the insurance company, but it would also incentivize customers to maintain a healthy lifestyle complying with drugs, dietary restrictions and exercise. It would ensure customer delight and in effect increase the insurance company's market share. Win-win situations in business don't get better than this.

Creating a Perceived Shortage

Make your customers run for your product by making them believe that your stocks are limited.

We have all encountered this statement, 'Limited discount offer ... till stocks last'. How many times do you believe this? Probably, never. But if Xiaomi (the Chinese mobile phone maker) does the same, many fall for it.

What is it that Xiaomi does differently? It announces a 'Flash Sale' a few months in advance. Xiaomi announces that it will sell its new model on say, 17 August 2019 during a 'two-minute window' on XYZ and abc e-commerce platforms. So in effect, the channel partner (the e-commerce platform) is equally responsible for promoting the upcoming sale. Xiaomi also ties up with social media platforms like Facebook, Weibo, etc., garnering more marketing muscle.

On the day of the flash sale, in order to be able to buy that highly hyped phone, most consumers stay logged onto the e-commerce sites for about 3–4 hours in advance. So the platform has a lot of eyeballs at that time. The banner advertisement rates on these platforms, at such times, are sky-high (I have heard about 20–25 times higher than normal). I am sure this bonanza is shared with Xiaomi too. So I have a sneaking suspicion that Xiaomi probably makes more money from the hiked advertising revenue than it makes from the actual sale of the product.

'Where's the win-win situation here?'

1. Xiaomi's marketing expenditure is low. Since the e-commerce platform is an equal partner, it subsidizes the promotional budget.

2. The e-commerce platform claims a substantial amount of the surplus advertising revenue.

3. Due to the very nature of the sale, Xiaomi is left with practically zero inventory at the end of that two-minute sale window. Which manufacturing company wouldn't be happy with this position (Inventories suck cash flow and drag down margins)?

4. The consumer gets a fantastic deal on the product, since a lot of resources and efforts spent on conventional promotional are minimum.

IMPRESSIVE IMPRESSIONS

Get over the conditioned mindset that says, business is a win-lose situation. We have been brought up on the thinking that, 'in business, for you to win, someone has to lose'.

That's *passé* now. To remain sustainable in the future, one has to scan the ecosystem, identify all stakeholders and then create synergies to build business models that help everyone's interests.

Creating win-win situations in business is easier than it sounds. Here are some key principles that will prove handy, when you think of creating win-win situations.

1. **Double whammy:** Milking both ends of the value chain, that is, making money from the consumers as well as the back-end service vendors.

   Where can one use this trait to build a unique business model?

   This trait, Double Whammy, can be used in sectors where you are running a business and you find that there is an opportunity of training people in sufficiently large numbers.

2. **Monetizing a third party's NVA:** Identifying someone else's NVA and helping them monetizing it.

Where can one use this trait to build a unique business model?

When you see an opportunity in a domain where there's a scope for a mass-consumption service and there's a lot of unutilized capacity in the supply chain. You can disrupt the incumbents (who have high sunk costs due to self-owned assets) in the industry with this model.

3. **Zero inventory of your own:** If you can help monetize someone else's NVA, then, as a corollary, you can do business with zero (or almost zero) inventory of your own.

4. **Fractional ownership:** Selling an asset to a group of customers.

Where can one use this trait to build a unique business model?

When you try to sell expensive stuff and finding single customers for the asset is tough, see if you can use this kind of a model.

5. **Service first, business later:** Offer your services first, even before the consumer pays you. Think about making her/him pay later. Trace the user journey before she/he buys your product/service and see where you can offer additional services to get them hooked onto your platform.

    a. **Aggregating competitors on a platform:** Bringing multiple competitors on a common platform and targeting a particular consumer segment

    'A smart way of using this approach' might be when you are trying to enter a highly crowded and hence, competitive market, where there already are too many players and capturing market share from each other is extremely difficult.

6. **Pay for what you use:** Don't charge the customer a penny more than the quantum of services she/he uses (no hidden charges).

An offshoot of this is 'compliance-based pricing'.

Where can one use this trait to build a unique business model?

When you have access to a technology that can monitor the tiniest fraction of usage of your service by the consumer.

OR

When the risk profiles/usage patterns of different customers vary widely.

7. **Creating a perceived shortage:** Making your customers run behind your product by making them believe that your stocks are limited.

   Where can one use this trait to build a unique business model?

   When you are entering a crowded market, this is a good way to:

   a. Create exclusivity

   b. Reduce your marketing spend

   c. Run a lean inventory model

   d. Launch limited edition versions of a product

SECTION 2

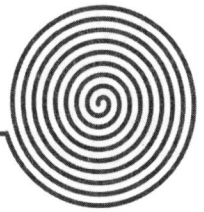

The Logic, Not Magic, Behind Innovation

Chapter 3

Last Mile User Connect

THE BEGINNING

Where does the journey of an innovation begin? Many say, it begins with a problem. But where does a problem originate from? A problem arises when there exists a user for a particular product or service. Would there be a problem if there were no user? Whether the user is a human being like a driver for an automobile or an inanimate entity like a bulb for the electricity service? So who comes first, the problem or the user? Of course, the user. One doesn't need Einstein's IQ to answer this question, right?

But do we always begin our problem-solving exercise with the user? More often than not, we begin with a particular solution or a technology in mind. We say, we have access to or control over XYZ technology, let us use it to create a breakthrough offering.

Is that the right way to approach innovation? Let us explore.

For over the last two decades, design thinking has been the discussed as a wonderful tool for making innovation happen, or for that matter to solve any kind of a problem (complex or simple).

DESIGN THINKING (DT)

DT is an approach to problem-solving that keeps the intended user of a product/service at the centre at all times (right from the stage of identifying the right problem to ideating for a solution to prototyping and testing of the solution). Hence, it lays enormous emphasis on user-centricity. DT encompasses people by observing them and gaining insights (through their behaviour patterns), ideating (brainstorming,

Figure 3.1. The Design Thinking Framework

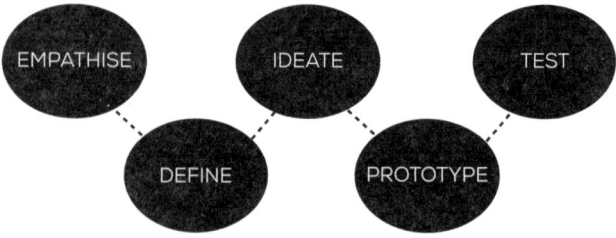

Source: d.School–Stanford

looking at a problem from multiple perspectives), iterative prototyping (visually/physically representing the thinking) and scenario building. A few decades ago, designers were brought in at the end of the product creation process to beautify the product by introducing some fancy aesthetics. Today, forward-thinking companies are involving design thinkers to answer the question, 'What to make?' rather than, 'How to beautify what is made?'.[1] This shift has happened because the high empathy quotient (EQ) of a design thinker helps her/him to quickly capture the latent, unarticulated needs of the consumer. The high EQ stems from the relentless emphasis on user-centricity as the main building block of DT.

Classically, the Hasso Plattner Institute of Design (commonly known as the d.school) at Stanford University captures the DT methodology in the five steps (Figure 3.1).

1. Empathize: Understand the user deeply. There is a bunch of techniques that a designer uses in this phase (more details about that later).

2. Define: Making sense from the data/information captured from the 'empathy' phase. Here, the problem gets defined and redefined from the user's perspective, rather than from the usual provider's perspective.

3. Ideate: This is the stage of generating possibilities to solve the defined problem(s).

---

[1] Tim Brown–CEO, IDEO, USA.

It's Logical: Innovating Profitable Business Models

4. Prototype: Here the ideas take the shape of a proof of concept (POC). Technological and other feasibilities are considered.

5. Test: Feedback is sought from multiple stakeholders and acted upon by redoing the prototype. This could mean going back and forth multiple times.

The entire process is iterative and keeps the user at the centre of the exercise.

Hence the probability of innovation to happen is the highest, using this approach.

If this process (DT) is followed well, consequently, the probability of obsolescence of your offering goes down substantially, since user feedback forms the backbone of the entire approach.

IDEO, the world's premier product design consulting firm and now an innovation consultancy, pioneered this methodology. IDEO's founder, David Kelley, was a professor at Stanford University, where he popularized this methodology.

Another design consultancy, Daylight Design, USA, uses simple terms to capture the essence of the DT methodology (Figure 3.2).

Figure 3.2. The Design Thinking Methodology

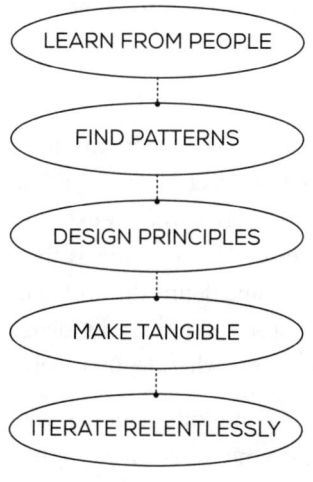

Source: Daylight Design, USA

Stanford	Daylight
Empathy	Learn from people
Define	Find patterns Formulate design principles
Ideate	Make tangible
Prototype test	Iterate relentlessly

Table 3.1. Similarities between the Stanford and Daylight Models

According to me, these words sound more relatable and easier to understand than the Stanford terminologies.

Learn from people, find patterns (from the data captured), design principles (criteria that the solution must meet), make tangible and iterate relentlessly are pretty much self-explanatory.

Similarities between the Stanford and Daylight models have been summarized in Table 3.1.

What I love most about the DT methodology is its relentless focus on the user. This relentless focus on the user, is what differentiates the DT methodology from other problem-solving approaches. That focus enhances the EQ of the solution generator multifold and that is where lies the key to making innovation happen.

EMPATHY

Simply put, empathy is the ability to be able to put yourself in someone else's shoes, to be able to feel what the other person is feeling. In creating innovative offerings, this is an extremely important trait that an innovator must possess. Because this is the ability that enables an innovator to understand and define the problem to be solved correctly. Otherwise, the innovator will invariably solve a problem that she/he thinks is the issue as against what the user feels.

Over the years, while consulting large companies as well as helping start-ups, for me, extreme user-centricity has translated into what I call as 'Last Mile User Connect'.

Figure 3.3. Ikon (1999–2003) 1.3 EXi

Without bothering about the definition of 'Last Mile User Connect', let us look at: What happens without 'Last Mile User Connect'? Once we see some real-life examples, the need for the definition will disappear.

Figure 3.3 represents the Ford Ikon that was launched in India in 1999. There were different versions priced between ₹5.25 lacs and ₹7 lacs. If you convert that money to today's value (considered at purchasing power parity-PPP), it would be around ₹40 lacs to ₹45 lacs. That kind of pricing, in 1999, positioned Ford Ikon in the luxury segment.

Typical to multinational companies entering an emerging economy back then, Ford decided to cut costs by creating an India-specific version of the car. When a car maker wants to cut costs, the first casualties are invariably some supposedly luxury features. One such luxury feature that got eliminated was that the two backdoors **did not** have 'power' windows, only the front doors did. Back in 1999, in India, a premium segment car was generally driven by a chauffeur. So the result of this cost cutting initiative was that the chauffeur driving the car had the luxury of power windows, while the owner, on the back seat, had to manually roll the windows up and down.

This is what I mean by not having the 'Last Mile User Connect'.

This raises an important question? Why did this happen? I can only conjecture the scenario.

Probably, the manager of the India Launch was given a targeted selling price and he had to cut costs to match it. He must have created a checklist and ticked off certain items, based on his own judgement or the collective judgement of his American team. They must have ticked off the power windows for the back doors. Were they wrong? From an American perspective, no, they weren't. In the US, the concept of chauffeurs doesn't exist, almost everyone self-drives. From Monday to Friday, a typical American drives alone. Even on a weekend, when the family travels together, kids below eight years of age are strapped into a 'safety seat', with no access to the doors. Most managers reach such decision-making positions (product launches in foreign countries) in their late thirties or early forties with kids who are eight years or less. Hence, the thought of power windows for the back doors seems redundant to such folks. And they must have eliminated the power windows for the back doors. So from their perspective, they weren't wrong. But they definitely missed that 'Last Mile User Connect', in the Indian context.

Many a time, this lack of 'Last Mile User Connect' is the difference between success and initial failure.

Let us look at another case of a blockbuster product not getting instant initial success.

Sharp Corporation was not the first one to launch the flat-screen plasma TVs (Figure 3.4), but they were certainly the first ones to create a big flutter in the market, with a blockbuster launch, somewhere in the first few years of this century. This TV was much better engineered and designed, had much better picture quality, was a lot more stylish than the then existing cathode-ray tube (CRT) TVs. On every count (except perhaps the sound quality), this technology beat the then existing CRT TVs. Despite all this, these TVs failed to make a dent in the market during the initial launch.

Figure 3.4. Plasma Screen TV

Why should this happen? Why should a highly superior product not be bought by consumers? A survey was commissioned to find why the sales of the TV had not taken off. Every surveyor was asked to go to people's houses to find why, rather than administer a questionnaire at the store. When you read below, the most common reason why people weren't buying this superior product, it will bring a smile on your face.

Back in those days, televisions hadn't invaded our bedrooms. A television would generally be found in the drawing room, proudly placed in a slot at eye-level, within a wall cabinet which also used to have a showcase and some storage space. This slot would invariably be square in shape to house the then popular CRT TVs (which used to be square). The new plasma screen TVs had wide screens and hence were rectangular in shape... would not fit into the existing piece of furniture. **That was the reason people were avoiding buying the superior plasma screen TVs.**

Can you imagine a sillier reason for why a better-designed, technologically superior, more user-friendly product failed to find acceptance in people's minds?

Simply put, people were not willing to change their furniture to fit in a new television. Understand that it is extremely difficult to change people's habits. It's so much better to design products and services that dovetail into people's habits rather than try to change them.

By now, you would have definitely realized what I mean by 'Last Mile User Connect'. The Ford Ikon and Sharp's Plasma screen TVs are classic examples of companies missing out on 'Last Mile User Connect'.

Now, that we have seen what happens without 'Last Mile User Connect'.

'Let us see what happens with "Last Mile User Connect"'.

I am associated with a few B-schools as a visiting professor. I take courses on strategic innovation, new product creation, new business model creation, entrepreneurship, etc. Across all these courses, one common assignment that I make the students go through is what I call as, Empathy Fortnight. I divide the class into groups of five students each and I assign a target segment to each group. The brief for the assignment is straight forward. 'Over the fortnight, each group has to spend time observing their respective target segments and come up with some new product(s)/service(s) offering for that target segment'. Let me tell you about one particular group's journey through this exercise.

This group's target segment was 'Hearing and Speech impaired housewives'. The group members came back to me saying that they were not able to find hearing and speech impaired housewives and hence, were not able to make much headway in the assignment. After a little discussion, all six of us (five of them and myself) sat down and made a list of families that we knew in our respective circles. Within the next 10 minutes, we had a list of about 180 families. We sifted through the members of these families and found that there were two women who fit the bill (hearing and speech impaired housewives). We then connected with those two families and sought their permission to spend some time with these ladies. Getting permission was not difficult because they were from our close family circles. We planned a visit to their houses. We chose a timeslot between 9.30 am to 11.00 am.

Why did we choose this slot? The reason was very simple. During that timeslot, a housewife is generally alone at home (children having gone off to school, the husband being away at work). Why when she is alone? Because we wanted to observe the housewife's behaviour when she did not have any assistance while going about her routine chores. To ensure this, we picked the days when the housemaid was on leave (during extreme situations, the researcher observes problems that would not arise normally).

Since the families were from our circle of acquaintances, entry into those households did not prove to be a problem.

In all, we spent about two and half to three hours at both these households. Among other observations, the following stood out:

1. When the doorbell rang, the lady could not respond.

2. When she put something in the microwave oven for heating and set the timer, she would wait in front of the oven looking

at the display. Why would she wait there for the entire timer duration? We figured her anxiety being that, if she went to another room to do something else and didn't get back on time to press the reset button, the oven would keep on beeping. She was aware that that she would not be able to hear the beeps and that the oven would keep beeping. This anxiety was holding her from attending to other activities during that particular timeslot.

3. When she put something in the pressure cooker, she would invariably hover around it constantly looking at her wristwatch. Why so? Over some gesticulated exchanges with her, we figured that she avoided being out of the kitchen when the food was being cooked in the pressure cooker, if she went to another room for another chore, she would miss the whistle of the pressure cooker (remember her faculty of hearing was impaired) and food would get overcooked. We could see a hint of helplessness in her eyes.

With these simple observations, my students created a wrist band (which the lady could wear) with an embedded bluetooth module (Figure 3.5). A similar bluetooth module would be embedded in the relevant home appliance.

The functioning would be as follows:

1. When the doorbell rang, the wrist band would vibrate, and a green LED would glow on it.

2. When the timer of the microwave oven timed out, the wrist band would vibrate, and a red light would glow on it.

Figure 3.5. The First Prototype: Wristband for Speech and Hearing Challenged

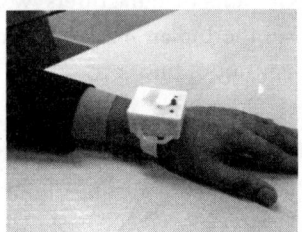

3. When the pressure cooker whistled, the wrist band would vibrate, and an orange light would glow on it.

   (on top of the wrist band, you can see different coloured LEDs)

Isn't that a simple product?.... Back in 2013, nothing like this existed.

One question to all my readers,

Where do you think this product idea got conceived? It is a no-brainer, right? We conceived this idea based on our observations during those 3 hours that we spent with the targeted user in her surroundings. 'In her surroundings', being the catch phrase. Anywhere else, we may not have caught the exact problems. That's what last.

Out of the five students working on this assignment, two were mighty thrilled with the outcome and wanted to explore the possibility of creating a company manufacturing such wrist bands. They asked me whether I would help them plan and execute their venture. I happily agreed. Just to test their seriousness, I told them that they should come back to me, in the next three to four weeks, with a sort of a roadmap about how they intended to move forward. They did their initial research and came back after about five weeks. When I saw them, I sensed a sense of despondency in both. They told me that there were two big issues they would have to tackle.

1. To start a manufacturing company in India, they would need fifteen plus licenses and acquiring these would take anything between ten months to a year (back then, in 2013, the government had low focus on 'ease of doing business').

2. The product that they wanted to manufacture was so very simple that it could be easily replicated. Within a few months of launch, Chinese manufacturers would get millions of similar units in the Indian market at probably half the price and drive them out of business.

These realisations meant that they would find it very difficult to sustain the business. They were dejected, but credit to them that they did not give up. We continued discussing about how we could take the idea forward.

THE BEAUTY OF THE BUSINESS MODEL

We were very clear that there was a strong unsatisfied 'user need' that we had identified, and we must not give up, just because manufacturing the device was going to be difficult for us. After three odd months of constructive brainstorming, the two of them came up with a brilliant *pivot*. They said that they would make the design of the wrist band open source ... any manufacturer who wanted to manufacture the wrist band would be free to manufacture it provided the wrist band had a bluetooth module embedded in it. They would create a software platform which would license out the application programming interfaces (APIs) to consumer appliance manufacturers, who wanted their products to be labelled as 'hearing and speech impaired-friendly'. This meant that the wrist band manufactured by any manufacturer (with their API embedded) could communicate with any consumer appliance (with their API embedded) (Figure 3.6).

With this tweak (pivot) in their business model, they would not only get over their own fear of manufacturing, but also access a much larger market. Imagine if they had gone with their initial plan of manufacturing the wrist bands. They would probably have sold a few thousand pieces before the Chinese would have taken over the

Figure 3.6. Wristband Connected to Home Devices via Bluetooth

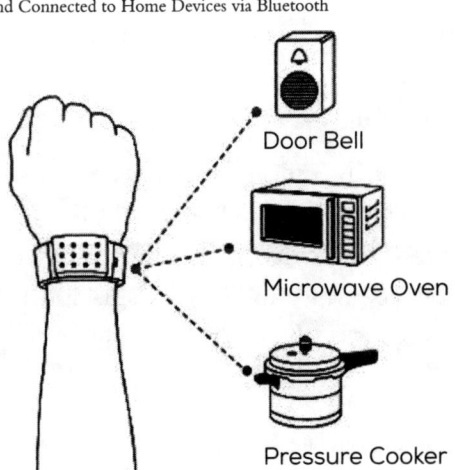

Door Bell

Microwave Oven

Pressure Cooker

market. Now, they could have access to the entire global market. The move from a B2C (business to consumer) to a B2B (business to business) model could be a game-changer. B2C for a start-up is tough considering the amount of promotional expense one has to incur for customer acquisition. For a B2B model, getting the first customer is difficult, but when acquired, it is a long-term connect. Moreover, when such a customer sells his own offering, your service gets sold too. Remember the concept of creating win-win situations?

The two entrepreneurs could go for something even grander. Try to get certifying agencies such as CE—Conformité Européenne (for Europe) and UL—Underwriter Laboratories (for USA) to make it mandatory for appliance manufacturers to embed the API, as a standard practice, to ensure that their products are recognized as **hearing and speech impaired-friendly**. If they succeed, just imagine the size of the market they would have access to.[2]

IMPRESSIVE IMPRESSIONS

'Last Mile User Connect' is oftentimes, the difference between success and initial failure. Understanding the user in her/his context is the most important act in your pursuit of making innovation happen.

1. Relentless focus on understanding the user will enhance the probability of making innovation happen.

2. Consequently, relentless focus on understanding the user will reduce the risk of obsolescence.

3. It is extremely difficult to change people's habits. It's so much better to design products and services that dovetail into people's habits rather than try to change them.

4. Be ready to pivot your business model based on the changing circumstances. Study the ecosystem carefully and look for

---

[2] Unfortunately, the students did not continue, they opted for an Ivy league higher education.

Figure 3.7. The Sweet Spot Where a Business Should Strive to Be

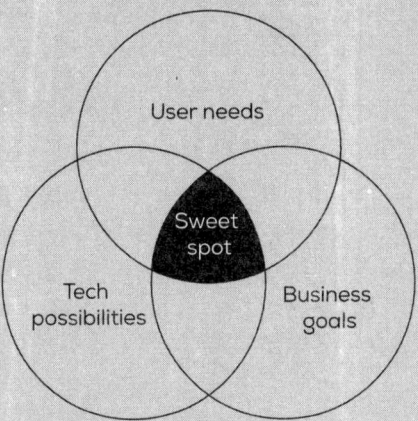

synergies and how you can piggy-back on some stakeholders while providing them value.

A sustainable business model exists at the sweet spot as shown in Figure 3.7. This is the zone where, the user needs are satisfied, the business has access to the technological possibilities to satisfy the user needs and its business goals too are met. If any of the above conditions are not met, then the business model needs to be relooked at. User needs have to be considered above all else. In the wrist band case mentioned earlier, the students had captured the user needs perfectly well. Their initial plan of manufacturing would not have satisfied their business goals (because of the threat of duplication due to low entry barriers). But they could overcome it by creating a platform from which they would license APIs to both, wrist band manufacturers and appliance manufacturers. With this business model, they would be at the sweet spot.

That's where every business *must* strive to be!

Chapter 4

Train Your Mind on the User

USER FIRST, TECHNOLOGY LATER

After having discussed about 'Last Mile User Connect', it is a good time to delve deeper into understanding the user.

In most companies, most of the time, the solution generation process begins with:

- What capabilities do we have?
- What technologies do we have control over?

Conventional logic says, the above are appropriate questions. They may be appropriate, but they are not the right ones in today's dynamic times.

Without getting into an intellectual debate over this, let us look at an example.

INNOVATION IN A SERVICE-BASED ORGANIZATION

A telecalling BPO was looking at 'enhancing the efficiency of the calling process'. The initial focus, as is the buzz today, was on 'digital transformation'. They were looking at enhancing the efficiencies of the various processes through the use of technology. The HR folks got in touch with DK seeking a proposal for a 'breakthrough ideation' workshop for enhancing the efficiency of the 'calling process'. To begin with they were insistent on having the workshop only for senior management (VPs and above). However, considering that there was a real problem to be solved, DK insisted on having the entire team involved in the workshop. A few back and forths later, it was decided that a team of 19 would participate in the workshop. This team comprised senior management, techies, solution architects and two telecalling executives (the ones who actually make the calls).

The workshop began with a 'hits and misses' session, where participants shared what they thought has worked and what hasn't in the past. This went on for a couple of hours. A lot of jargon was being thrown around. Many 'quality of service (QOS)' goals were being discussed. DK noticed that the two telecalling executives (hereinafter referred to as TCs for brevity) had not uttered a word throughout the discussion.

During the first break, DK made it a point to sit with the two TCs over coffee to make them voice out their observations, since they were the ones who were in actual touch with the end user (the prospect who they would call). After some goading, one of them mentioned, 'All these high level discussions are fine, but when I pick up my headphones and speak to a prospect, I can sense whether she/he is interested in our offering or not "on the basis of her/his voice tone".' This was a cursory statement by him, but it was a loaded one. It was a trigger for innovation to begin. A new metric for enhancing the efficiency of the 'calling process' had been casually mentioned by someone at the lowest rung in the hierarchy (but more importantly, the only rung in direct contact with the end user).

As the participants reassembled after the break, DK asked the concerned TC to repeat what he had told him during the break. DK insisted on exploring this observation further. Initially, this parameter, namely 'voice tone', was treated as too subjective to be useable at scale. The argument being, every TC's judgement would be different and it would be impossible to standardize the process. One of the VPs said, 'We have 3,500 TCs making around 50 to 70 calls per 8-hour shift, which cumulatively translates to 175,000 to 245,000 calls per day. If we were to take the subjective judgement of every TC, it would be impossible to run our operations.' DK insisted on holding the negatives at bay for a while and delve a little deeper into possibilities. With a little prodding, the techies in the team said, 'Voice is basically a sound wave that has frequency, wavelength and amplitude. And these parameters are perfectly measurable.'

The team then focused on how one could quantify the 'voice tone' of a prospect's response. Finding a technology to make this happen became the focus of the innovation effort. The brief for the solution generation process emerged as:

'Can we recognize voice tone patterns and correlate them with the outcome of the call?'

The company had a repository of recorded call logs of a few million prospect calls made over the previous eight years (recollect the 'Your call may be recorded for training and quality purposes' disclaimer that we usually hear when we speak to a customer service executive?). The outcomes (whether converted or not, if converted then the duration of time taken for conversion, number of repeat calls required, etc.) of these calls too were documented in the archives. Over the next seven months, an algorithm was built to understand the relationship between the 'voice tone of a prospect' and the outcomes achieved. Lo and behold, co-relations between voice tonality and outcomes emerged from the archived call logs. Painstaking analysis led to the emergence of clear patterns in the co-relations as follows:

1. Voice tone pattern—1 → Outright 'Yes'
2. Voice tone pattern—2 → Maybe 'Yes'
3. Voice tone pattern—3 → On the fringe of 'Yes' and 'No'
4. Voice tone pattern—4 → Maybe 'No'
5. Voice tone pattern—5 → Outright 'No'

Many iterations later, the final solution unfolded as follows.

A self-learning algorithm was created. This algorithm analyses the voice of the prospect during a live call. When a call centre executive makes a call and the prospect responds, the prospect's voice is fed to the voice analysis engine in real time. Within the first 12 words uttered by the prospect, her/his 'voice tone' is analysed and the prospect gets slotted into one of the above mentioned five categories. All this happens in real-time (during the conversation between the

TC and the prospect). The category to which the prospect belongs to is displayed on the screen in front of the TC and the relevant conversation flow (questions to be asked) appear onscreen, facilitating the TC to have a meaningful and effective conversation.

All this leads to better targeting of the marketing and sales efforts, reducing the cost, time and efforts required in the sales cycle. The prospects who are inclined towards the 'NO' categories get directed to other sales channels and are approached differently (not through the calling process), hence no more pesky calls for such people.

P.S. This company did not have the requisite technology in-house. They searched around in the start-up ecosystem and found a couple of them dabbling in the appropriate kind of speech recognition tools, collaborated with them and the result is there for all to see. Hats off to their perseverance!

Now, time for a question:

Did DK and the team start with a technology in mind at the beginning of the problem-solving exercise?

No, they did not. Initially, they just focussed on the user, the need for an appropriate technology emerged later.

This is what I mean by 'user first … technology later'.

Compare this with the points I made at the beginning of this chapter, namely 'In most companies, most of the time, the solution generation process begins with:

- What capabilities do we have?
- What technologies do we have control over?'

Had the call centre stuck to this conventional approach, they would not have been able to come up with the breakthrough.

However interesting this example might sound, there will be enough people who will quote two visionaries:

Henry Ford: 'If I had asked people what they wanted, they would have said faster horses.'

OR

Steve Jobs: 'We don't do any market researches because customers don't know what they want until we've shown them.'

Let us decode Henry Ford's words first.

The commonly available mode of mobility back then was horse carriages. That's what people were aware of. So, if one were to ask people directly, they would invariably say, 'We wish we had faster horses.' The visionary in Henry Ford realized that the core need of people was speedier mobility and not faster horses. He married that need, namely 'speedier mobility', with the then new technology (the automobile) and innovated on the manufacturing process (the assembly line, interchangeable parts, etc.) to make it affordable for people. The crux of the matter is Henry Ford understood the underlying, unarticulated need of 'speedier mobility'. He did not have to conduct any conventional market research for that. He understood the user more than the user understood himself at that time.

Now, over to Steve Jobs.

Jobs never believed in asking people directly what they wanted. But he was a very keen observer, who understood users' existing habits, routines, belief systems, pain points while handling devices. He had a highly perceptive intellect that asked questions of existing technologies as to how the user's interactions with these devices could be simplified. He then pushed his technology teams hard to simplify these interactions. Apple products would not have been what they are without Jobs' relentless focus on 'user experience'.

So do you still feel, Ford and Jobs did not bother to understand their users?

Henry Ford, later lost it when he insisted that, he would let the customer choose any colour as long as it was black. And paid a heavy price for his stubbornness in the 1920s, when Ford Motors lost substantial market share to GM and others. That's when Ford lost focus of his users.

IMPRESSIVE IMPRESSIONS

For creating breakthroughs, focus on the following:

1. User

2. User

3. User

1. **User first ... technology later.** Do not get enamored by technology. Begin the problem solving process by focusing on the user and not with an attitude of 'which technology should I use to overcome this challenge?' Remember you have to understand the problem first and to understand that you have no option but to begin with the user.

2. **Try to find new metrics for enhancing service quality** levels rather than just attempting to utilize new technologies to enhance efficiencies of existing metrics. The 'User first' approach will help unearth these new and untried metrics. That's where the magic lies. 'Do not ignore "Qualitative" metrics because they appear to be immeasurable at present.'

3. **Don't give up on wild ideas** (as a corollary to point number 2). However, crazy the idea of using 'Voice Tone' as a metric sounded initially, it did see the light of the day.

4. **Involve people with diverse backgrounds in the problem-solving process.** Remember, the trigger for innovation came from the telecalling executives and then was built upon by the techies in the team. If there were no techies in that team during the workshop, that trigger may have been shelved as being 'too subjective to be used at scale'.

5. **Collaborate and co-create.** The company did not have the requisite speech recognition technology in-house. They were open to explore the ecosystem and it took time for finding the right partners. If it were not for their 'willingness to experiment', the idea would have suffered a quiet death.

Chapter 5

Don't Just Sell What You Make; Make What Might Sell!

Let's delve deeper into this 'user first, technology later' conundrum discussed in the last chapter with another case.

This one is right out of DK's crystal ball.

Somewhere in 2007, DK was approached by a company in the pharmaceuticals business. This is a large multinational with operations across the world. Their problem statement was, 'What should we be doing in 2030?' DK thought to himself, 'What a weird question? Are they joking? Looks like they are pulling a fast one on me.' DK didn't discuss much further. That evening, he made a passing reference to his wife, about this company's demand. She had spent 26 years in the pharma industry, heading the sales and marketing functions for three pharma companies in the latter half of her career. She did not seem amused with what he told her. Across the dining table, she explained to him the workings of the pharma industry. From initial drug discovery to the marketplace, back then, it generally took around 15–18 years (sometimes even more). She added, with such long development schedules, what the pharma company was asking was a logical question. With this reassurance, DK recommended his dialogue with the company.

INITIAL APPROACH AND THE 'LOW-HANGING' FRUIT

DK's first question was, 'What is the intent of engaging me?' The CEO responded, 'We want to be a major player in the globe by 2030.'

'Is that it? Or is there anything else?', DK asked.

DK could sense the quizzical look on his face.

The marketing head chimed in, 'Our R&D has some blockbusters in the 'anti-diabetics' pipeline.'

DK nodded, turned towards the CEO and asked, 'Do you want to be the leader in the anti-diabetics segment or you want to be a major player in the pharmaceutical industry?'

The marketing head was quick to interrupt, 'What do you mean? We are the leader in that segment now and that's the market we understand best. We also have a presence in Sartans and are at the cutting edge with trials on for Odilorhabdins (ODLs). So that's where we obviously would want to be.'

The CEO, getting a drift of what DK was asking, responded, 'Yes, we want to be a major player in the industry.'

'Alright, help me get some answers here.' DK said, 'If you want to be a major player in the industry then we need to look at the market first and then at the capabilities we have. DK asked one more question, 'Which is the segment that consumes the most medicines?'

'Senior citizens', was the obvious response.

DK continued, 'Then, let us focus on them.'

With average lifespans increasing, the population of senior citizens (60 plus years of age) too would rise worldwide.

A look at the World Bank population data,[1] released in 2007 said:

The number of senior citizens above 60 years of age will increase fivefold to 1.4 billion from 275 million in 2007.

So, by 2030, senior citizens would comprise approximately 16.5 per cent of the global population.

A similar report about the rise of diabetes patients by International Diabetes Federation,[2] revealed the following:

[1] https://data.worldbank.org/indicator/SP.POP.65UP.FE.IN
[2] https://www.ncbi.nlm.nih.gov/pmc/articles/PMC3068646/

In 2007, there were 246 million diabetes patients worldwide. This number would likely rise to 380 million by 2025.

'Which is a better market to focus on … if you have to be a major player in the global market?' DK asked the CEO, who glanced at his team. The marketing head avoided eye-contact.

The CEO took the call, 'We need to look at the market for senior citizens.'

Then DK took off, 'Let us make senior citizens the focus of our research then.'

Along with the team, he began studying their lifestyles. As the sample size increased, the profile of a typical senior citizen emerged as follows:

1. A senior citizen would increasingly be living independently (alone or with only the spouse for company) because the family structure is breaking down rapidly even in lower-middle income countries. Many a time, the children are located in a far-away town (domestic/overseas).

2. Typically, consumes five–eight tablets at a time, maybe twice a day for various ailments.

3. Is losing memory.

4. And remembering to take medication on time is a challenge at times.

5. Has no one to monitor her/his therapy.

6. Is a retired individual, hence non-earning. Lives in a suburb that maybe far away from a hospital.

7. Their children or (immediate family) who do not live with them are constantly worried about their health and whether these elderlies have taken their medicines for the day or not. There's a regular phone call exchange to check on that.

A round of medicines for a senior citizen is shown in Figure 5.1.

So a big challenge for these people is compliance of therapy. Missing any medication is rather risky for them.

Figure 5.1. A Round of Medication

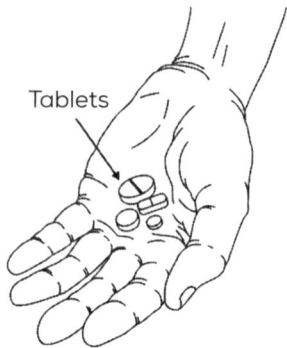

Tablets

DK's question to the team was:

'With this understanding, should we not "shift our focus from new drug discovery to ensuring compliance"?'

New Drug Discovery ➔ **Ensuring Compliance**

Among the team, there was a lot of chatter, 'But that's not our core competence and we would be straying away from what we know and do.'

DK did not relent. A little deeper understanding of the target group (TG) revealed the fact that certain types of ailments occurred as clusters in this segment, e.g. high blood pressure, cardiac disease, diabetes. Hence, the person's daily therapy would comprise 'a statin, a sartan, a metformin and a clopidogrel'.

More observation of the TG revealed that while consuming these medicines, she/he would have to remove these pills from their respective strips one by one and that sometime or the other, the individual would forget one of the tablets. Considering this, DK's first question was,

'How can we improve convenience to enhance compliance?'

The obvious answer: by reducing the burden of remembrance. If an individual has to take five tablets at a time, she/he has to tear them off from five different strips.

Figure 5.2. A Composite Tablet Strip

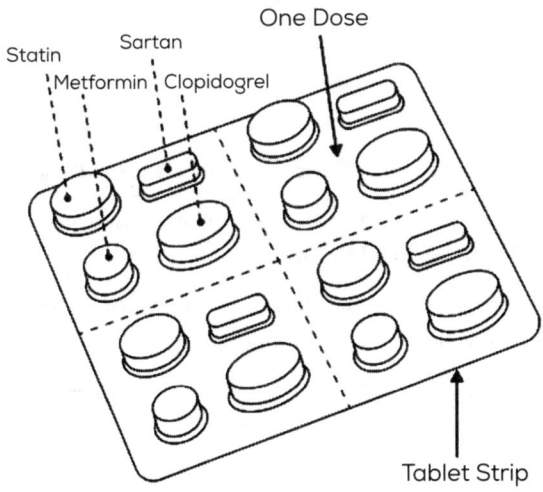

The first suggestion was to incorporate all the necessary tablets in one strip, that is, 'a statin, a sartan, a metformin and a clopidogrel together in one strip' as shown in Figure 5.2.

This would reduce the inconvenience of having to remove four tablets from four different strips. Just one cut and all the four tablets would be accessible. This way, we could reduce the burden of remembrance and enhance the ease of storage too. This company did not manufacture all the drugs. Hence, it would have to create strategic tie-ups with relevant manufacturers and perform the final tableting operation in their own factories. The final strip would be shipped from the client's factory.

The objection raised by the team was: every patient consumed medicines of different strengths (some 0.5 mg, some 1 mg, etc.). This would create a lot of chaos on the tableting lines.

This was a very justified objection. On discussing with doctors, DK realized that there would be about five–six such combinations for different patients. A modern numerically controlled tableting machine could easily handle these combinations without any loss of speed. So this was perfectly doable. Once successful with one cluster of ailments, the same combo-strip could be adopted for other clusters of ailments, necessitating more tie-ups with relevant manufacturers.

This was indeed a low hanging fruit that could be exploited immediately. A consumer would definitely prefer this convenience.

The Second Thrust and a Slightly Futuristic Scenario

Now that, the focus had shifted from 'new drug discovery' to 'ensuring compliance', DK intended to move ahead at full steam.

'Ensuring compliance meant that the number of times one has to remember had to be brought down.'

So the *focus* of the problem-solving exercise had to firmly remain on 'reducing the occasions of remembering'.

Were there any methods to make that happen? 'Extended-release pills' are capable of releasing a drug into the body at predetermined, constant rates.

Extended-release pills have the following obvious advantages:

1. Since one has to take such a pill less often, many a time only once a day, it ensures easier and better compliance.

2. They are safer for consumption, since they maintain a constant drug concentration in the body and consequently have fewer side-effects.

The discovery of such drug delivery mechanisms dates back to 1938 (patent awarded to Israel Lipowski). The technology has seen numerous upgrades since then. However, till date, the extended release mechanism has been used to deliver one drug over at a time.

Can it not be made possible to deliver multiple drugs over a period of time?

This question needs to be explored further. If this becomes possible, then the above-mentioned patient could make do with one extended release capsule which contains a sartan, a statin, a metformin, a clopidogrel and has multiple layers within, to release these throughout the day in the required concentrations. For example, at present, the patient consumes four tablets (a statin, a sartan, a metformin and a clopidogrel) at a time, twice a day, then:

Can the proposed extended-release capsule not have four compartments (for the four different drugs)? Each compartment being programmed to release the relevant drug at the right time. For the last decade or so, research has focused on polypills—capsules that are capable of carrying and releasing multiple drugs over a period of time.

The Third Thrust and a More Futuristic Scenario

With the extended-release capsules, one can reduce the frequency of taking medicines from two/three times a day to once a day. DK thinks the burden of remembering has to be reduced even further to ensure better compliance.

Is there any technology available to make this happen? **Yes**, there are nicotine patches that people use to keep off cigarettes. There is research being conducted to make one single patch last for a week/fortnight. Today, this patch can deliver only one drug into the body.

'DK envisages a single patch delivering multiple drugs into the body (at safe concentration levels) over a week or more.'

Current advances in nanotechnology and material science could definitely turn this into a reality.

'DK's advice to the client (back in 2007)' was that they should also invest in researching and creating 'extended-release multi-drug delivery mechanisms' rather than only focus on 'new drug discovery'.

'The logic being' that the duration of the 'new drug discovery' cycle might be longer than that of creating 'extended-release multi-drug delivery mechanisms'. And hence, the latter would yield faster business results. It would help capture the senior citizens' segment quicker than the competition.

The target customers would remain loyal because of the convenience of compliance.

It is unlike DK to stop thinking once the ideation stops. He looks at all the scenarios of failure too.

Since the focus of this problem-solving exercise is compliance to therapy and reducing the occasions of having to remember, DK asked, 'What is the extreme case of forgetfulness?'

'The obvious answer is a patient with Alzheimer's disease'.

Imagine such a person, living alone or with an equally aged spouse.

He said, today if a senior citizen forgets to take a pill, she/he misses only one drug, but with the proposed multi-drug delivery system, what if she/he misses one pill or one patch? That would be a disastrous situation. The children (living far away) of such senior citizens are forever worried whether their elderly parents are consuming the prescribed medications regularly and on time or not.

So, to ensure compliance for a person with extreme memory loss, an external care-provider has to be brought into the picture. There are a lot of care-providing agencies in the market today. 'Can they be roped in?', was DK's question.

'With this thread of thought, DK proposed the following model to be adopted by his client'.

The pharmaceutical company should tie-up with multiple care-providing agencies. The family whose parents live alone, could subscribe to this service. There should be a mobile phone-based platform. The children (or relatives who want to keep track of the therapy compliance of the parents) would be registered on this platform for receiving notifications.

A caregiver from the network would visit the subscriber's house, administer the medicine to the parents and update the information on the platform (Figure 5.3). The registered family members/relatives would instantly get a notification. Thus, the fear of their parents missing out on regular medication, would be assuaged. The medicines administered (by the care-giver) ould be:

1. At present, the regular pills from different strips.

2. In the immediate future, from a consolidated multi-pill strip.

Figure 5.3. Notification Platform for Medicines Administered

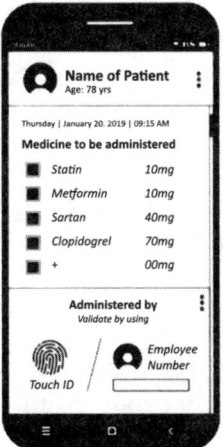

3. Maybe four to six years into the future, a single extended-release polypill once a day with all medicines.

4. Maybe nine to ten years hence, a single patch carrying the medication for a week or even a fortnight.

For such a service, there would be an immediate market and would give the client company immediate access to their current and potential consumers (i.e., senior citizens). It makes for a strong business case. There would be families who would sign up today itself.

Plus, for the advanced multi-drug delivery systems (when introduced), the band of loyal customers would be created from today itself. DK envisaged the service when he looked at the behaviour of Alzheimer's patients, however, there exists a use case for normal senior citizens too.

Most importantly, this is a business that would have a much shorter break-even period and a much deeper penetration in the long run.

The beauty of identifying and creating win-win situations.

IMPRESSIVE IMPRESSIONS

Relentless focus on the user segment leads to completely different yet strong and futuristic business cases. Good enough to stay ahead of competition? There is **no magic** to create breakthroughs, **it is pretty much logical**.

1. **In the age-old debate of 'core competence v/s what the consumer seeks', the latter is the clear winner in today's VUCA (Volatile, Uncertain, Complex, Ambiguous) world.**

   Conventional management focusses on what the company can do best and it strategizes based on what they are capable of doing. Hence the company tries to sell what it produces. But is that what the consumer wants?

   Companies must subscribe to the motto: 'Don't just sell what you make.... Try to make what might sell.'

   Sounds weird, right?

   But think about it, if you sell what you make without paying heed to what consumers are seeking, you may meet your immediate sales targets but may not remain sustainable in the long run. But if your quest is to constantly try and figure out what the consumer wants and there is a willingness to adapt, then your company will remain sustainable in the long run. In the above quote, I have used the word 'might', for a reason. Because despite the best of efforts in understanding the user, there may be an occasional failure. But get this clear: The failure would not occur due to your relentless effort in understanding consumers, rather it would be due to some wrong interpretations about the consumers or inadequate implementation.

   If the pharmaceuticals company (cited above) focused only on the 'anti-diabetics' segment (i.e., their current core competence), it would aim to access only the 380 million diabetes patients by 2030, whereas if it sought to explore what their existing consumer needed beyond anti-diabetic drugs, 'it would stretch its efforts to access 1.4 billion senior citizens plus younger diabetes patients by 2030'.

'Which pursuit would lead them to become a major player?' The answer is obvious, isn't it?

2. **Keep stretching the limit and you will land up with breakthroughs.** The collaborative model with the care-providing agencies did not get conceptualized out of thin air. Only when DK pushed the limits of lack of compliance of therapy by senior citizens, he asked the question, 'What is the extreme case of forgetfulness?'

The obvious answer emerged, 'A patient with Alzheimer's disease'.

And from this obvious answer, did the collaborative model involving the 'pharmaceuticals company and the care-providing agencies' emerge.

Once again, DK is teasing us with his favourite question, 'Is it magic or logic that lead to the above?'

All our lives, we have been brought up on a staple of playing safe by focusing on the precept of $\mu \pm 2\sigma$ (mean $\pm$ two times the standard deviation).

Remember the bell curve (Figure 5.4) and those statistics lectures.

Figure 5.4. A Typical Bell Curve

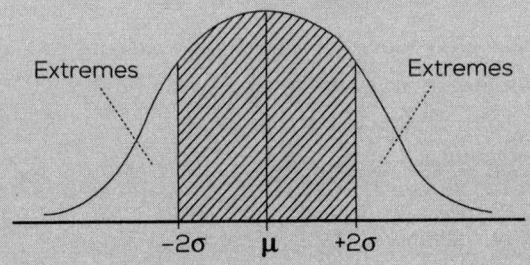

We were mostly told to focus on the $\mu \pm 2\sigma$ (at the centre of the curve) and treat all the data points falling outside that zone, as 'outliers to be ignored'. We were repeatedly told the range that fell within '$\mu \pm 2\sigma$' is our 'representative sample' and we must focus on that. Weren't we?

But, in the above case of the pharma company, if DK had ignored the outliers, namely 'patients with Alzheimer's disease', would he have come up with the collaborative model? Pretty unlikely.

3. **Oftentimes, the outliers give voice to what the medians want, but are unable to verbalize.** Hence, 'do not ignore the outliers'. The needs and wants of the outliers will make your offering more holistic and hence, more desirable for the medians too.

4. **Moreover, it would give you 'pointers for creating multiple versions of your offerings to segment your target market'.** It is then up to you to figure out how you penetrate the various segments, with different strategies.

5. **A business model should never be cast in concrete.** As the concept evolved, a completely different business model evolved for the pharmaceutical company (collaboration with care-giving agencies, which can be implemented right now itself). This could happen only due to DK's unwavering focus on the end-user. Despite the proposed technological advances in 'multi-drug delivery mechanisms', DK never lost focus of his **real** pursuit of **ensuring compliance** by **simplifying** it **for the consumer.**'

'Be open to tweak your business model.' Keep scanning the ecosystem for synergies with various players and of course yes, DK's favourite mantra, 'look for creating win-win situations'.

Chapter 6

Gamifying User Research

So far, we have discussed the significance of relentlessly focusing on understanding the user. Now, let us move onto exploring *how to understand the user?*

Are there any tools/techniques that one can follow?

Let us begin with an actual project.

In the summer of 2011, Sassi Vadapav was launching its chain of 'vadapav' stores in Mumbai. Vadapav (Figure 6.1) is the Indian version of the burger or is the burger the Western version of the vadapav? I don't quite know. That is beside the point.

A 'batata vada' ('vada' for short) is a potato dumpling, rolled in a thick batter of 'gram' flour and deep-fried to an appetizing golden-brown ball. This 'vada' is then put into a squarish-round piece of locally baked bread (Pav), laced with some tangy 'chutney' (liquid/powdered mixture of different Indian spices and herbs) ... all in all, an amazingly mouth-watering affair. It is Mumbai's favourite, 'on-the-go' finger food (as in, one does not need to wash one's hands after eating it, just a few swipes with a tissue are good enough). The vadapav has made its presence felt in other Indian cities and towns as well, albeit, not with the same penetration as in Mumbai.

Figure 6.1. A Spicy Vada Pav

All over Mumbai, one can savour this delight, doled out of roadside carts or 15 sq ft kiosks. It is a highly unorganized, fragmented business.

Sassi Vadapav's co-founder, Sunny Swami was very smartly trying to aggregate that demand into a consolidated stream by launching a chain of outlets, maintaining the highest standards of hygiene and quality to match those of any multinational fast food chain, such as McDonald's.

Sunny had realized that he would have had to create an experience around the humble vadapav to hold sustained consumer interest to achieve his dream of creating a pan-India chain of finger-food outlets. To do that, he planned to add a few variants and a choice of beverages along with the vadapav.

While Sunny himself was passionately involved with the kitchen in the development of variants of the vadapav, he was well aware of providing the right kinds of beverages at Sassi's outlets. Sunny wanted an answer to the question: 'What beverages would go best with vadapav?'

Sunny reached out to DK with this query and asked, 'Would you help us out with this research?'

He shared a 'scaled' questionnaire (that his team had already created) to probe what people would prefer to drink after gorging on a vadapav. The questionnaire incorporated all kinds of questions to elicit responses about the beverages involved.

He asked DK, 'Can you ask your some of your students to run these questionnaires with the segments of consumers that we have identified?'

After hearing him out, DK responded sarcastically, 'If all your research questions are ready, why do you need me?'

Swami responded sheepishly, 'With your access to students, we could get this done faster.'

DK said, 'Alright.' Without any further discussion, they bid goodbye.

For projects received in the colleges where DK teaches, as is his usual practice, he circulated details about this project among his students, asking if anyone wanted to participate. Eleven of them responded and they became a team.

The team met one day, at the campus to discuss on how to take this assignment forward. DK has an instinctive apathy to questionnaires. His students too, know how he abhors questionnaires as a tool of user research. He firmly believes that no one (yes, no one) answers a questionnaire honestly and hence the data so collected is redundant for decision-making.

After an intense brainstorm, they formulated a unique methodology.

They created a kiosk with two separate sections, insulated from one another. A visitor would enter through the first section and exit through the second one after engaging in the planned activities. The separation between the sections would be such that, a person in either section would not be able to see or hear whatever that would happen in the other one. These kiosks were branded with Sassy's colours. Sassy's staff manned them in their regular, bright uniforms.

The team set these kiosks up at three different locations in Mumbai city:

1. Outside Churchgate Railway Station (the last station at the southern tip of Mumbai), to capture the office-going crowd.

2. Outside Andheri station on the west side, to capture the upper middle-class crowd (from Lokhandwala complex) and the huge number of students in that locality due to the presence of large educational trusts such as SVKM (NM and its sister colleges) and Bhavan's Group of Institutes.

3. At the state transport (ST) bus junction opposite Mumbai Central station, to capture the slightly lower middle-class crowd.

Visitors were enticed into the kiosk with an offer to enjoy Sassi's delicious vadapav at no cost ... yes, absolutely free, under one condition: They would have to play a game with the team.

After having relished the vadapav, the visitor would move to the second section of the kiosk, where there was a simple game laid out.... Like the one all of us would have played as a kid at a fair.... The game where one would be given a bunch of rings to be thrown around a

Figure 6.2. The Preference Game

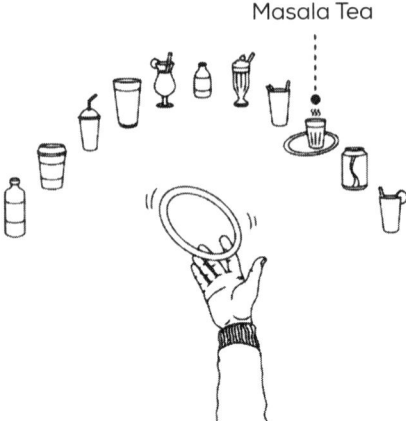

Masala Tea

range of goodies (biscuits, chocolates, stationery items, soaps, etc.), laid out on a table a few feet away (Figure 6.2). One had to throw the rings on the objects that one wanted and if you could toss a ring around an item, that item would be yours to carry....

In this section of the kiosk, different beverages were arranged in a semi-circle, equidistant from the point where the visitor (player) would be made to stand. The player was then given a bunch of 10 rings and asked to throw the ring around the beverage/s of her/his choice. Any item successfully 'ringed' would be offered to the player as a drink (prize money). The students were posted as observers (at all the three locations). They kept a meticulous record of the players' actions:

1. Which beverage would the player attempt to 'ring' first?

2. How many times would the player attempt to 'ring' the same beverage?

3. Which would be the second, third, fourth, fifth ... beverage that the player would attempt to 'ring'? and how many attempts on each?

4. After having successfully 'ringed' a beverage, would the player attempt further 'ringing'?

5. If yes, which beverages?

And many more such details were logged by the student observers. General demographics of the visitors too were noted.

THE LOGIC

The visitor, after having eaten the hot, tangy, spicy vadapav, would obviously want to have something to drink. Which drink? The visitor herself/himself was demonstrating her/his preference through the 'ringing' game.

The team recorded 904 footfalls in all (across all the kiosks), over a week. The recorded data was collated and analysed.

'The most preferred beverage that visitors at the kiosks, were attempting to 'ring' was piping hot Masala Chai (tea brewed with ginger, clove, nutmeg, etc.)'. This was completely contrary to general expectations that after having eaten a hot, spicy vadapav, one would want to drink something cold.

'This exercise was carried out in the month of May (peak summer in Mumbai).' Hence, the bias that could be attributed to cool weather for the 'Hot Masala Chai' choice was not a factor.

This was in complete contrast to what Swami and his team had expected. But the result was a true reflection of people's choice. Why?

In the game that DK's team made people play, the situation was **real**, that is, the player had just eaten a hot, tangy, spicy vadapav and was wanting to have a drink. The player was most likely to attempt to 'ring' what she/he wanted to drink at that moment. So, unconsciously, the player was exercising her/his choice out of free will, and hence demonstrating her/his **real** preference. The student observers were meticulously noting the sequence of these attempts. Hence the collated data clearly threw up what consumers **really** wanted after eating a Sassi Vadapav.

Note:

Before setting up the game, the team had referred to some articles on 'gaming principles' to understand how to create an unbiased game, for example:

1. Having the same level of difficulty for all choices by keeping the beverages in a semi-circle, equidistant from the point of throwing.

2. Eliminating player's ability bias: If a player is right-handed then the possibility of her/his attempting the beverages on the right side is higher. To avoid this, the team would rearrange the beverages after every visitor.

3. And more such…. Not stating them here, because this is not a book on setting up games.

IMPRESSIVE IMPRESSIONS

Gamification as a tool for user research is extremely effective as it reflects the **real choice/preference of the user**.

Why so? When people play a game, they are at their competitive best, either against themselves or their rival. When we are involved in a game, our behavioural guards are completely down … our only aim is to achieve a favourable result. The focus on the task at hand is complete and there is the least possibility of any bias creeping in. And at such times, people let their **real self** surface out.

1. When the **real self** surfaces, **people exercise their innate choices/preferences**.

    We have to create settings where this can happen and tap for insights into user behaviour.

    The latent/unarticulated needs of the consumer manifest in such settings and those are the **seeds** of **new opportunities**.

2. Observation Research can be more creative than **just observation**.

Get creative with your user research. Create 'appropriate gaming experiences' to tap user insights.

3. A warning: Be contextual, don't generalize, for example, in the above case, the exercise was done in Mumbai and the most preferred drink emerged as Masala Chai. If the same exercise were to be done in say, Delhi or any other location, the result may be completely different. So honour the cultural context of the user.

Does conventional consumer research throw up such unbiased data?

DK has made his views about questionnaires amply clear earlier. Hence, I won't elaborate further. Even focus group discussions (FGDs), if not conducted well lead to biased results. In an FGD, when there are multiple participants involved, there is a tendency (on the part of the participants) to make statements that are aimed at making themselves appear different from what they actually are (socio-economic status, compassion quotient, etc.). Unless the moderator of the FGD is a seasoned researcher, such biases are difficult to catch. Many a time, I have seen even seasoned professionals faltering when it comes to identifying **real** motives in an FGD.

Depth interviews have a better chance of success. However, they too cannot eliminate biases completely. People don't let all their behavioural guards down … ever.

The next time when you want to understand your users, 'think multiple times' before you appoint that fancy consumer research agency for insight-mining. Get your own and your team's creative juices flowing first. Think of an appropriate game to garner deep insights. Enjoy the experience! After all, the darkest zone is right under our own nose.

Chapter 7

The Bull's-eye Question

When we want to understand the consumer, we want to know a lot of things about that individual. During depth-interviews, a researcher tends to ask too much. Rather than evoking the subject's response about the issue(s) involved, it is the researcher who keeps probing relentlessly. The interview then gets directed by the researcher rather than evoking the subject's stories. Sometimes this leads to the subject feeling her/his privacy compromised and the responses don't remain genuine.

Hence, it is essential that the researcher formulates one question that would get the subject talking and narrating experiences around it. That is the one question that DK refers to as '**the bull's-eye question**'.

Even in the case of 'observation studies', this approach helps identify the central action/activity to be observed. Otherwise, it becomes too overwhelming for the researcher to keep track of everything that is happening around. It is important to narrow down on that central activity which is at the root of it all.

Let me tell you about some real bull's eyes.

1. COMMUNITY-BASED INVESTMENT ADVISORY

A few years back, DK was approached by an Indian conglomerate that wanted to enter the investment advisory market. An investment advisory is a company that provides investing advise to individuals in exchange for a fee.

The challenge statement was, 'How can we enter the market differently and capture substantial market share?'

On this assignment, six of DK's students were working with him. Generally, when DK works with a team, he briefs the team members about the client expectations in detail and then leaves them to ruminate on the brief for a week or two. They do not even meet each other during the 'rumination' period, lest they speak about the project and bias each other's thinking. DK prefers that everyone thinks independently during this period. Invariably, the team comes up with brilliant ideas and methodologies to approach the challenge. After the pre-determined 'rumination' period, they meet and brainstorm intensely, dissecting as well as building on each other's ideas. These brainstorming sessions, many a time, extend to a few days before they finalize the methodology. All his clients know this process and by now, have realized that it is time well-spent and not time wasted.

DK's students met him after four weeks. They were in the last semester of their MBA programme and very keen on equity markets. They had generated an exhaustive report on the various investment options and their corresponding yields generated over the previous 15 years, namely:

- A comparative analysis of the yields of various mutual funds
- A comparative analysis of the equity market returns of various industry sectors
- A comparative analysis of the Fixed Deposit (FD) rates offered by companies belonging to various industry sectors
- and many more.

DK was mighty impressed with the meticulous technical analysis. He spent a good thirty minutes going through that report. It was a gold mine of information for an investment advisory. He lauded their efforts.

With a poker face, he continued, 'What is the challenge statement? Is the client asking our advice on how they should invest their client's funds? **or** Are they asking us how to capture market share? Your analysis is a wonderful input for the former question but the latter one should be approached differently. Plus, they would have seasoned analysts for the technical analysis. They don't need us for that.'

What determines market share? Consumers, right? So to gain market share, we have to capture the imagination of the consumer. How do we do that? By understanding what she/he desires, correct? It is as simple as that.... Well, easier said than done.

DK asked his team, 'Why would a person seek out an investment advisory? To maximize the return on her/his savings, right? So fundamentally, what business is the advisory in? **Helping people maximize the return on their savings**, correct? Are you with me?'

The students nodded in agreement. There was no denying DK's logic.

'So let us find out **why people save money**?' DK continued. 'Once we know why people save money, automatically, we will know why they would seek advice from an investment advisory.'

'Hence, our research has to lead us to answer the question, **why do people save money**?'

'Do you agree?'

Remember, I told you, no one can deny DK's logic.

DK went on to tell his team, 'In all our user interviews, let us keep our conversations around this one central question, **why do you save money**? And let the subject take over from there. "We should only prod and not probe". We should not compromise on the demographic data; we must capture that meticulously. But please do not begin your conversations by asking for the subject's demography, let it emerge during the conversation. You may prod appropriately.'

DK and his team did many role-plays among themselves and some friends to get the conversation flow right. They wanted to make sure that the interviews would not get too intrusive and yet they would be able to get the requisite information. Gradually a broad conversation template emerged. This exercise continued for a few days. Once, DK was convinced that all of them were on the same page, he said, 'Now let us begin the user interaction.'

All through this, the client displayed enormous patience, albeit grudgingly.... DK's track record stood in his favour.

Thus, began the next phase of the research. DK and his team began asking people, why they saved money. The demographic data that emerged about the subject was being captured meticulously. Since a lot of rehearsals had gone into the conversation flow, the template of information collection was more or less common across the team. Many a time, qualitative researchers have a tough time documenting data.

As the sample size increased and the team began to share information from their respective interviews, interesting patterns began emerging. Here are some:

'India is a country with multiple communities within. There are many ethnic groups that display varied behaviour. But the reasons why they save money are more or less the same among the urban population (which was the target segment). There are about 21 reasons why people save money, and these are common across communities. Some are listed below:

1. Planning to get married

2. Planning childbirth

3. Buying an asset: a car, a house, etc.

4. Child's post-graduate education

5. Child's marriage

6. Planning an exotic vacation

7. and many more.

The team, in their next round of interviews, also looked for differences across communities. And what emerged was extremely interesting.

'All these communities displayed different parameters for the above identified reasons for saving money. The following explanation will make it clear (the numbers mentioned below are an indicative average and may differ in reality).

In a Tamilian family,

- The average age at which the boy gets married is say, 31 years and 2 months.

- The average age at which a girl gets married is say, 26 years and 1 month.

- The first child gets born at the father's age of around 34.

- A couple, generally, moves out into their own nuclear home, somewhere between marriage and childbirth.

- General expenditure on a child's wedding is ₹X,XXX,XXX.

In a Marwari family,

- The average age at which the boy gets married is say, 23 years and 9 months.

- The average age at which a girl gets married is say 21 years and 3 months.

- The first child gets born at the father's age of around 25 years and 1 month.

- They generally live in a joint family.

- The decision of purchasing a house is taken jointly by the elders in the family.

- General expenditure on a child's wedding is ₹YYY,YYY,YYY.

Corresponding numbers for the Bengali community were say,

- Boys' age at marriage 28 years and 5 months

- Girl's age at marriage 25 years and 4 months

- First child born at the father's age of around 31 years and 3 months.

- The couple, generally, moves out into their own nuclear home, somewhere between marriage and childbirth.

- General expenditure on a child's wedding is ₹Z,ZZZ,ZZZ.

For a Maharashtrian family, the numbers were say,

- Boys' age at marriage 27 years and 11 months.

- Girl's age at marriage 25 years and 7 months.

- First child born at the father's age of around 29 years and 2 months.

- The couple, generally, moves out into their own nuclear home, somewhere between marriage and childbirth.
- General expenditure on a child's wedding is ₹A,AAA,AAA.

And so on, for different communities.

DK's team then mapped the 21 reasons for which people save money onto the above demographics and obviously realized that 'each community had different requirements from their savings at different times in their respective lives'. The dataset emerged as depicted in the accompanying table.

Milestone in Life	Tamilian (Father's age in years)	Marwari (Father's age in years)	Bengali (Father's age in years)	Maharashtrian (Father's age in years)	Community 5	Community 6
Child's PG education	55–56	45–46	52–53	48–49	_____	_____
Child's marriage	65 (in case of a boy child) 60 (in case of a girl child)	50 (in case of a boy child) 45 (in case of a girl child)	59 (in case of a boy child) 54 (in case of a girl child)	56 (in case of a boy child) 54 (in case of a girl child)	_____ _____	_____ _____
Amount required	₹XXX,XXX	₹Y,YYY,YYY	₹ZZZ,ZZZ	₹A,AAA,AAA		
Milestone 3	_____	_____	_____	_____	_____	_____
Milestone 4	_____	_____	_____	_____	_____	_____

And so on, for other milestones and other communities. As the sample size of the survey increased, the above-mentioned patterns began crystallizing even more. The final dataset included information about eleven major communities that live in the city of Mumbai.

With these findings, DK approached the investment advisory.

'Does this make sense to you? Does it tell you something?' (Most advisories give blanket investment advice based on the age, income class and other such standard information).

But if one focusses on the above information, it will lead to a more personalized community-specific investment advisory. That way the investment advice would be tailor-made to suit a customer's requirements better. And hence, ensure a higher market share.

IMPRESSIVE IMPRESSIONS

Finding that absolute core question is key to a successful 'Consumer Insight' exercise. That is the **bull's-eye** that a research team has to strive to get to. The rest of it will automatically fall in place.

1. Getting to that bullseye question is not difficult. Once you have got into the consumers' shoes, you have to crystallize what's that one thing at the root in the consumer's mind. After a lot of discussions, the team in the above case, arrived at that one question, **why** do people save money?

2. Follow the KISS (Keep it Simple, Stupid) principle. At the beginning of the formulation of the research approach, do not bring in too many parameters. The other parameters will gradually emerge if you have got the bullseye question right.

3. Give your researchers some 'me-time' to crystallize the client brief and ideate independently. DK gave his team a brief and then let them be for a few days. In fact, he says that he avoids meeting the team lest they end up talking about the project brief and bias each other's thinking. If you think this goes against a collaborative approach, think again. The team sat together after that 'rumination' period, to intensely brainstorm for dissecting as well as building on each other's ideas. Researches cannot be rushed into a project just because the client wanted it yesterday.

4. A good research methodology too needs a pilot before rolling it out. Remember, DK and his team did a sizeable number of role plays, not only among themselves but by involving some outsiders too. With these rehearsals they became aware about a lot of surprises that could crop up in actual research interviews and based on this, they finetuned their conversation flows. This enabled the team to arrive at a more or less common template to be followed by different members of the team. In qualitative research, a broadly common template is essential, because individual researchers have their own styles and invariably end up capturing disparate bits of information which are next to impossible to coherently transcribe. The 'rumination' period mentioned above, followed by the intense brainstorms, ensured tremendous learning from each other, which helped the team arrive at a fairly common template.

2. A CUSTOMER-FRIENDLY BANK LOSING CUSTOMERS FROM SPECIFIC BRANCHES

With the Investment advisory case, we looked at a strategic issue of looking at your core offering and then structuring it properly. Now, let us look at how to formulate the bull's eye question when targeting a specific problem area.

Remember the days when we had to visit a bank personally to transact (enquiring/applying for an auto loan, buying foreign exchange, getting a demand draft made, etc.).

In 2010, an aggressively growing private bank approached DK with a peculiar problem. They had 11 branches in the city of Mumbai, three of these were losing customers. The other eight were growing.

The bank was known for its high customer focus and heavy investments in enhancing customer experience. Despite this, three branches were losing customers. They had analysed the issue from various angles (a few aspects were as follows):

- Did the unhappy customers belong to any specific demography?
- Were there any co-relations between their credit card spends and repayment patterns?
- Any failed transactions at the bank's ATMs?
- Any complaints against their respective relationship managers?
- And many more such specifics

Despite this, they were not able to put a finger on the exact cause of the undesirable customer churn. The head of Mumbai operations approached DK for a diagnosis.

As usual, DK floated the project among his students, 13 joined in.

Post some brainstorming after the customary 'rumination' period, the team came up with an extremely simple methodology, 'Let us capture the customer requests that were being turned down.'

How was this to be done? By now, you all must have got to know DK's aversion to the use of direct questioning. The process gets interesting hereon.

DK divided the 13 students into four groups. Three groups of three members each and the fourth one with four members.

The three groups with three members were deployed at the branches that were losing customers while the four-member group was sent to the branch which was doing well (i.e., gaining customers). That was to be the control group.

The branch managers at all the four branches were told to let the students be around in their respective branch offices. They were assured that the students would not interfere with the banks' operations. They would just be around as silent observers. The students would be restricted from accessing the safe-deposit vaults enclosure and other such high security zones.

The brief to the students was pretty straight-forward. They were to be in the branch observing the interactions between bank employees and customers.

They had to note down every time a bank employee said 'No' to a customer request and jot down the reason for the 'No'. In other words, every time a bank employee said 'No' to a customer request, the student would put a tally mark with the reason for the customer's request being turned down.

All this was to be done discreetly. It was tough in the beginning, but in my view, youngsters always manage to find a way.

Examples of some observations are as follows:

1. While withdrawing cash, if a customer at the teller's counter got it in the denomination of ₹1,000 notes and requested the teller to give him the money in the denomination of ₹500 notes instead and the teller didn't have that, he would say, 'No, I don't have ₹500 notes. Sorry, please accept ₹1,000 notes.'

2. If a customer went to a counter to ask for an application form for an automobile loan and if the executive at the desk, pointed towards another counter and said, 'No, that form is not here, please go to that counter.'

3. If a customer walked in saying, 'I am travelling overseas next week, I want to buy some dollars' and an executive replied, 'No, our branch doesn't have forex facility, you will have to go to our main branch.'

All such above instances were considered as a 'No' to a customer request. This exercise was conducted over two working weeks. When DK and the team put together all the data captured in the form of tally marks, what came out was beyond shocking.

In the three branches that were losing customers, on an average, a bank employee said 'No' to a customer request a whopping 33 times in a day.

Let us understand the magnitude of this finding. If a bank branch had 10 employees, then 330 customer requests were being turned down every single day.

The corresponding number for the fourth branch (the one showing growth in its customer base) was eight 'No's.

Does the difference in number of 'No's not tell the story?

Could there be any other reason why customers were turning their back on the three branches?

When all the reasons for the 'No's were collated, there emerged 19 different categories of reasons why a bank employee said 'No' to a customer request. DK's team shared the tabulated dataset with the three branch managers in their next meeting. Within about three hours of analysis, all the three managers concluded that 11 of these categories could be taken care of then and there itself, with a little bit of training to the staff and some restructuring of the bank's layout. All the managers concurred that this simple training could be managed from their discretionary budget for operational upgrades at the branch level itself, that is, they would not need any approvals from higher-ups. For the remaining, eight categories, the managers said they would need budget approvals from the divisional/regional levels.

What 'restructuring the layout' meant would be clear with the following narration:

One of the instances cited above was, 'When a customer asked for an application form for an automobile loan, the executive at the counter responded by saying, "Please, go to that counter", directing the customer elsewhere'.

Analyse the following situation carefully.

What the executive meant was that the particular application form that the customer wanted was not within his arm's length and it would be easier for the customer to walk across to the relevant counter rather than the executive getting up to get the form for the customer. The executive was not being discourteous, but it was just too much for her/him to get up every time a customer asked for something which wasn't around at an arm's length. A little bit of change in the layout of the furniture at the branch could ensure that all of the most commonly sought paperwork would be within arm's length of the front desk executives (at least). A little analysis of the frequency of customer requests gave a clear indication of which forms need to be placed where. It was that simple and straight forward.

All these findings led to improvements in the other branches (the better performing ones) too

What's the moral of the story here?

Once again, this highlights 'cutting through the riff-raff and getting to that one thing that you want your user research to focus on.'

IMPRESSIVE IMPRESSIONS

1. Spend time on getting to the essence, it is always time well-spent.

    How did the team arrive at the crux, that is, 'Noting down the 'No's uttered by the bank employees?' In the 'rumination' period, the team could not think of too many unique ideas, however, they were all at consensus about the need to spend time at the actual site, rather than crunch data at the desk. Still the methodology was not clear. All of them felt they were far away from that **bull's-eye.** Finally, after a few hours of brainstorming, they concluded that they needed to understand more about the customer service domain.

    The team then pored extensively over literature on QOS goals for customer service. After distilling all their notes, over endless cups of coffee, they came to the logical realization that in the domain of customer service, 'An individual does not like to be at the receiving end of a denied request'.

    A request denial, when understood in simple terms, means being faced with a 'No'.

Isn't that a logical conclusion?

But to arrive at this, rather simplistic truth, it took DK's team almost a week.

Armed with this realization, the team focused on finding the reasons for 'customer requests met with a No'.

2. Be prepared for surprises that crop up during the user research.

Please note, counting the number of 'No's was not the initial aim of the exercise. It was just a hygiene requirement that DK had stated. The team had never imagined that the occurrence of the 'No's would be so high. Many a time, qualitative researchers tend to read patterns too early in the data-gathering process and change track quickly. While this may work sometimes, but many a time, it scatters the initial focus. If the initial 'rumination' is done well, oftentimes, course-corrections are not required, since things were anticipated well before-hand. While this is DK's observation, it may not always hold true.

3. User research has to happen where the action is. The observations made by DK's team would not have happened anywhere but the bank branches. No number of questionnaires or focus group discussions would have thrown up the reality. If getting to the actual scene is difficult or impossible, simulate it as close to reality as possible.

Be creative with the simulations. Remember the ring game with Sassy Vadapav?

Chapter 8

Memetics and User Psyche

What is memetics? It is the study of memes, *so what is a 'meme'?* Richard Dawkins, in his book *The Selfish Gene* (Chapter 11), has explained as follows:

Examples of memes are tunes, ideas, catch-phrases, clothing fashions, ways of making pots or of building arches. Just as genes propagate themselves in the gene pool by leaping from body to body via sperms or eggs, memes propagate themselves in the meme pool by leaping from brain to brain via a process which, in the broad sense, can be called imitation. When you plant a fertile meme in my mind you literally parasitize my brain, turning it into a vehicle for the meme's propagation in just the way that a virus may parasitize the genetic mechanism of a host cell.

Simply put, memetics is the study of 'cultural heredity', similar to how genetics is the study of 'physical heredity'. How 'genes' are responsible for carrying forward our physical characteristics from generation to generation, similarly, 'memes'[1] are responsible for transmitting our behaviour to others. The noun, 'meme' has its origin in the verb, 'to mime', which means to imitate. Thus a 'meme' is a unit of behavioural imitation.

---

[1] Please do not mix the above definition with what passes around as a 'Meme' on social media these days. The above is a classical understanding of the term 'Meme'.

Why do some catchphrases stick in public memory while others just fade out? Why do some trends catch on and snowball into huge cult-followings, while others wither away as if they never existed?

How can memetics help capture actionable user insights?

Let's dive into DK's experiences. It was August 2010, with just two months left for Diwali, the festival of lights that all of India celebrates, Mr. Ram, Head of Operations at Nurture Group (NG) retail was facing the usual problem.

Close to festival times, Nurture Group, India's home-grown retail chain and the country's largest, used to stock delicate handcrafted artefacts, yummy savouries gorged upon in Indian households. All these items would be sourced from a network of self-help groups (SHGs). The SHGs are a very unique phenomenon in a lower-middle income country. A group of women, usually from the lower strata of the society come together under a more enterprising lady from their own community, manufacture various items like some handcrafted artefacts, pickles, papads (hand-rolled fritters) or savouries like *chakali, chivda,* etc. Different SHGs specialize in different items. These groups then seek out finance from various microfinance institutions or co-operative banks in their surroundings to run their operations. Microfinance is a very typical form of lending, where small amounts are distributed to people who are considered un-bankable by conventional banks.

These SHGs, invariably, comprise women who are typically school dropouts or have never been to one.

The purchase transactions between NG and these SHGs would never be seamless. The women would not keep the stock records properly, would not manage their inventories well, resulting in delayed deliveries. They would invoice items wrongly at times. Their accounts records would not be maintained properly, and the problems went on. These were issues that Ram faced every year around that time.

In short, 25–30 per cent of Ram's time would be spent on sorting out these issues. So he approached DK and asked him whether he could create a short training module on 'Fundamentals of Management' for the SHG women. With a little training in basic management fundamentals, the SHG ladies would manage their operations better and that would reduce his headaches.

Ram's initial thoughts were that, DK would put together a folder with the relevant content, within a few days and hand it over to him for training.

DK said, 'Ram, let us visit a few of those SHGs to understand the ground reality, what are the issues that they face? So far, I have only heard your side of the story. Let me understand the issues from their side too.'

Ram said, 'What is there to know? I have told you what I need.'

DK responded, 'That's true Ram, but there is always the other perspective. I would like to visit a couple of these SHGs sometime in the coming week. I will take some of my students, it will be a good learning experience for them, and we could get some fresh thoughts.'

Ram agreed, though a bit reluctantly.

Within the next few days, Ram arranged visits to two SHGs. DK, along with two of his students, visited Dharavi Bhagini Udyog Mandal (DBUM) and Sri Laxmi Khadya Udyog (SLKU), both, vendors of NG, located in Dharavi. Dharavi is a slum in Mumbai and is recognized as the largest of its kind in Asia. Numerous such SHGs function out of the shanties in Dharavi. These SHGs are involved in a wide spectrum of activities ranging from manufacturing of handicrafts and snacks to leather goods to stripping of consumer electronics for recycling.

The three of them made their way through the narrow alleys of Dharavi, bustling with activity. They spent the day interacting with everyone at both the SHGs. These conversations were not just restricted to their business and operations. DK had instructed both his students to engage in getting to know the lives of those people. To understand their motivations in life, their aspirations, their frustrations, etc. In addition, they chatted around with the community too: some housewives, some workers from neighbouring manufacturing units.

Back at DK's office, in the evening, the three of them exchanged notes well into the night.

When all observations were jotted down, one very basic understanding stood out and that was: "'However illiterate an Indian is, mythological stories are strongly etched in her/his mind, irrespective of the religious background". Even if one may not be able to read or write, these stories, narrated by parents/grandparents during one's childhood are firmly ensconced in the mind and can be recalled easily, not only due to their morals, but also for the vivid imagery. Generally, these stories have their roots in India's two classics, the Ramayana and the Mahabharata.'

'Hmm…, Let us read these classics. Do you have some English translations?', DK remarked nonchalantly.

Both looked at DK as if struck by a bolt of lightning.

Jaws ajar, they asked in unison, '*What?*'

'Yes, let us read those. If that's what connects with our audience, then let's see what we can use out of these classics', quipped DK. 'Let us look for stories from these classics that encapsulate management fundamentals that we are trying to explain', he continued, 'I know for sure that C. Rajagopalachari's English translations will make a good read. Let us each read them up and meet after three weeks. Read it in detail and be attentive to the nuances that may be useful to us for creating our training module.'

On the appointed day, three weeks later, they met to brainstorm. Each one had a long list of notes. An animated discussion ensued. Interesting insights were shared and few relevant stories, which could be used for explaining the principles of book-keeping and inventory management, emerged. Here are two of DK's favourites:

1. 'According to the Hindu belief, when one dies, Lord Yama, the god of death takes charge and carries the dead to his palace before dispatching them to either heaven or hell. At the entrance to the palace is Chitragupta, the record-keeper. At his table, Chitragupta, always keeps a large book of records, which is essentially an up-to-date list of the good deeds and the bad deeds committed by the dead person in her/his life. The dead one is dispatched to Hell if the bad

deeds outweigh the good ones and if it is the other way around then the dead one is transported to heaven.'

'Now, there you go, this story can be used to teach fundamentals of accounts', summarized DK, 'After all, can credit and debit not be analogies for good and bad deeds respectively? Isn't that big book of Chitragupta's similar to a ledger that accountants maintain? Let us use this story to make the SHG folks understand how to maintain accounts. Income is like the 'good deeds' and expenses are like the 'bad deeds. What say?' He couldn't hide his excitement.

Another interesting story from the Mahabharata that emerged was:

2. 'The Mahabharat epic is a tale spanning many generations with extremely intriguing subplots. One such important subplot (in fact, the main one) was the animosity between two sets of cousins, who were collectively referred to as the Pandavas and the Kauravas, respectively. The Pandavas were the righteous ones, who portrayed the good in society; the Kauravas were the scheming ones, who depicted the evil in society. The kingdom of Hastinapur was divided among the Pandavas and the Kauravas. The Pandavas, by virtue of their valour and righteousness, expanded the kingdom and were loved and respected by their subjects.' 'The Kauravas, on the other hand were abhorred by theirs. Jealousy took root and the Kauravas schemed and plotted to get the kingdom of Pandavas. They called their cousins for a game of dice with the condition of winner takes all. The game was cleverly manipulated by the Kauravas to ensure their own victory. The final stake was the kingdom, which the Pandavas lost. The Pandavas had to hand over their kingdom to the Kauravas and go into exile. Having agreed to the terms of the game earlier, they had no choice but to accept their fate. The terms were harsh. They had to spend the next 12 years in exile and 13th one, incognito. The condition being that, if, in the 13th year, they were recognized by

anyone, they would have to remain in exile for the next 12 years. With the Pandavas dispatched into the forest on their exile, the Kauravas led by Duryodhana, the eldest among them, went about exploiting the subjects of their newfound kingdom.

Meanwhile, in the forests, the Pandavas roamed around the country like hermits. They utilized this time away from the worries of politics, to devote themselves to propitiate different gods and acquire a host of celestial weapons, termed as *Divyastras* (meaning all-powerful weapons). They had the foresight to imagine that these weapons would be useful in their war with the Kauravas (which they would inevitably have to fight, since they were certain that the Kauravas would not honour their word of returning their kingdom after completion of the exile).

Twelve years passed by and the Pandavas had collected an arsenal of these weapons. The 13th year was approaching and the Pandavas were planning about how to stay unrecognized for the entire year, lest they be exiled for the next 12 years. They realized that even if they disguised themselves well, the celestial weapons that they would be carrying, would give away their identity. Hence, the obvious alternative for them was to hide these weapons in some safe place.

Wandering around in the Himalayas, Arjun, the third eldest of the Pandavas, came across a grove of Shami trees. The Shami tree is unique in structure, it has a slender trunk with a large, dense canopy of branches. The Pandavas decided to hide their weapons on the top of these trees, in the thick foliage, away from any roving eye. They carefully packed the weapons in linen and hid them on top of the trees and began descending the Himalayas.

When they had walked a little distance from the Shami grove, Arjun voiced a question, 'How are we going to locate these trees when we get back next year to retrieve the weapons?' So all the brothers retraced the path to the grove and began to climb down the mountain again. As they descended, they left some discreet markers along the way. They painted some boulders in different colours, engraved the barks of a few trees along the way. All of these, were meant to be permanent clues, cryptic enough that only they could figure out the next year.'

DK and his students, concurred that this was a great story to impart the fundamentals of inventory management. Storing raw materials, semi-finished goods in containers of different colours, keeping simple cards on each container to be filled in with every addition/subtraction from the respective container (much like the 'Kanban' system of the Japanese). So easy … to make the SHG folks understand practical tracking of material flow and the inventory.

'Proper inventory management would definitely help the SHG folks adhere to their shipment dates, Sir', chirped one of the students in a sing-song tone.

DK took charge and said, 'Yes, now let's go to NG and their SHGs and conduct the training module.'

He called up Ram and fixed a time to visit two SHGs to conduct the module. DK insisted that this time the SHGs should be different from the ones they had visited earlier.

On the appointed day, the three of them, accompanied by Ram and his executive assistant Saurabh went to Dharavi. The students narrated all the stories and explained the relationships with accounts, inventory, material flow, etc.

All of this was purely verbal in nature except for a couple of papers on which, there was a rough template of the supposed Kanban cards and the accounts book. They finished each module in 65 minutes flat at the two SHGs and returned, extremely pleased with the day's job.

DK was satisfied and commended both on a job well done. He expected that Ram would call the students again to deliver the module at the other SHGs. Three weeks passed by with no word from Ram. DK was disappointed and a wee bit angry that Ram had not even displayed the courtesy of thanking the students for a job well done. He called up Ram and gave him a piece of his mind over the phone and demanded, 'Why have you not called the students to deliver more training modules at other SHGs? You saw what a good job they did last time. The audience too loved it.'

Ram, a little embarrassed about not having communicated, responded, 'DK, I am sorry ... I really am but listen to me. You know ... after your students delivered the module at the two SHGs last month, the folks who attended got so excited with the content, that they themselves went to other SHGs and conducted the module almost verbatim. The others lapped it up and my troubles with the schedules have dropped drastically' and added timidly, 'Hence, I did not call your students.'

DK was stunned to hear this, too overwhelmed to say anything. He thought to himself, 'That means the audience imbibed the learning so well that the taught became the teacher and the original teacher became redundant! Wow! This is the best I have done in any consulting assignment I have ever taken up. What can be a better result than this?'

IMPRESSIVE IMPRESSIONS

Immersive ethnography can lead to fantastic breakthroughs, where no amount of conventional knowledge works. The insight that, 'No matter how illiterate an Indian is, mythological stories are firmly embedded in their heads', is such a strong meme in India.

DK and his students capitalized on this meme so effectively.... If DK's team had known about the meme that, 'No matter how illiterate an Indian is, mythological stories are firmly embedded in their heads', they would have been able to cut down a lot of time from their field research.

Hence, understanding memetics should be an integral part of any manager's arsenal. Anyone who wishes to understand consumer behaviour, must study memetics.

Memetics helps understand and predict upcoming trends in society and a manager must be able to foresee these. Communities behave in a particular manner because they share a common culture. If one wants a certain response from a certain community, a certain stimulus will have to be provided. When to use which stimulus, is a result of deep cultural studies. Memetics is a science that would help greatly in doing this. Companies need to inculcate the study of memetics in their 'managerial training modules'. A working knowledge of memetics always triggers the right direction for a research team.

To understand memetics better, read the next section. It should clear the concept of memetics and its utility in reading social trends that businesses could do well to follow. After reading it, do dwell upon the period between 2009 to 2013 and see what has actually happened on the ground in tier 2, tier 3 and tier 4 towns across India.

WHAT CAN CORPORATE INDIA PREDICT BASED ON MOVIES?

- Why is it that some organizations consistently outsmart and outperform their competitors?

- What is it that makes them come up with what consumers just seem to lap up?

- Do they do something special … consistently?

- How can anything special be done consistently? That's an oxymoron!

These organizations seem to have the pulse of the market at all times.

They always seem to be in a position to anticipate trends and create offerings (products as well as services) to service them.

How do they do it, is the big question.

A not very state-of-the-art field of study, memetics seems to be catching the fancy of some organizations who wish to get into the mindscape of the consumer before any competitor gets to know about what's going on in there.

Can memetics help figure out these trends before they become really big?

How these trends become big and catch the fancy of the masses is best left to academicians and psychologists. **Enterprises need** to be in a position **to know** that these trends are catching up and act on this knowledge before anyone else does.

Where could these leads (that some trends are taking root in public imagination) come from? This, according to me, is the big question.

Every country/society has a **popular culture** that is unique and it is the best indicator of what's happening or what's coming. A major part of popular culture in India is reflected by the following determinants:

1. Films that we watch. The success/failure of a theme projected in a movie is generally a direct metric of the acceptance/ rejection of that concept by the general movie-going public.

2. Cricket (Other sports too seem to be catching up of late).

3. Television soaps.

4. Festivals.

5. Politics.

6. Food/popular cuisine.

7. Fashion.

If we follow these broad categories that define popular culture, we could be in a position to identify undercurrents in the behaviour of people, which may snowball into trends at a later date. I would like to share a simple method that I have been following that seems to work.

Step 1: Take seven sheets of a large chart paper (as shown in Figure 8.1).

Step 2: Title each sheet with a category from the seven determinants of popular culture listed above.

Step 3: Begin listing out a couple of major events in that category every week along a timeline. By 'major

Figure 8.1. Trend Mapping

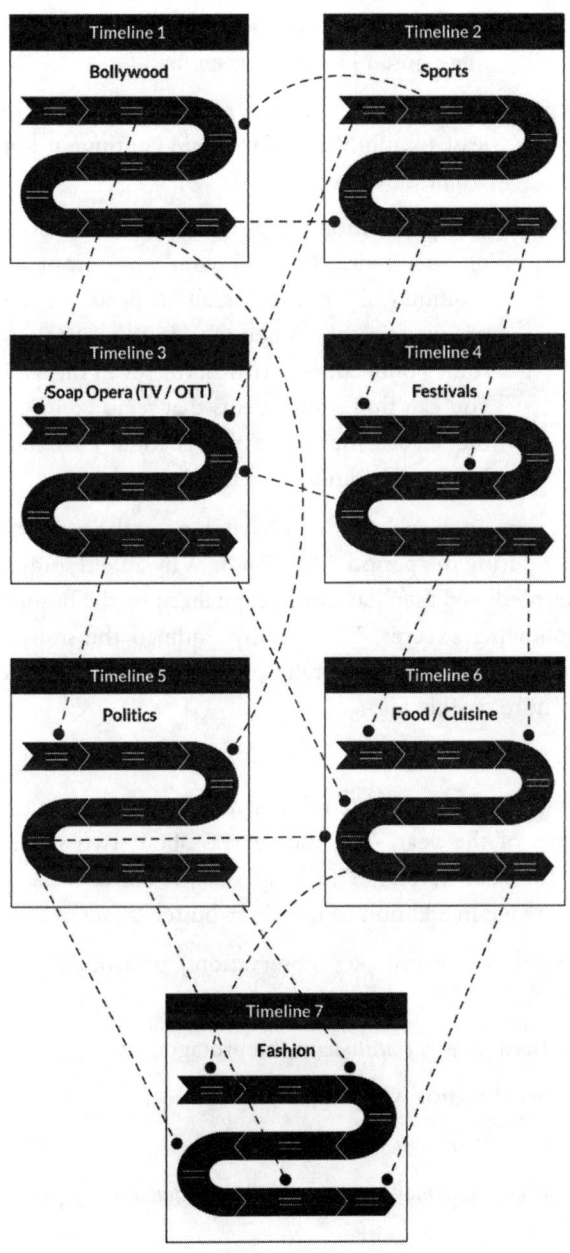

events', I mean something that is different/unique and stands out from the mundane. You need not detail these, just a broad gist is enough.

Step 4: Continue this process religiously for a period of at least six months. If you could continue it longer, that would be better.

Step 5: Every six months, keep these sheets side by side on the floor. Read all your posts from a standing position (this ensures that all the posts can be glimpsed simultaneously). When you do this, keep a watch for some connections across all the seven sheets. I am sure you can find some events that seem connected across the sheets. Join these events using pins and threads. You will begin to spot trends.

I will share one such analysis that I have done in the past. It is a study conducted during the period 2005–2008. Why an old study? Because the trends predicted then have been capitalized by the business world. In the following excerpt, I have only outlined the study, without going into details, only a few relevant events have been mentioned (not the entire weekly log).

Event 1:

The movie *Bunty Aur Babli,* released in May 2005, was one of the biggest hits of the year. The movie was about two small towners wanting to make it big. The song *'Chhote-chhote shaharon se …'* was quite a rage in addition to the chart-buster *'Kajra re'.*

Depicted below is a gist (key observations) of a mind map around *Bunty Aur Babli:*

- *Devil-may-care attitude* of the protagonists
- *Small towners* with big dreams
- *High aspirations*
- *Wanting to make a statement/become famous*
- Guts

- Hit songs such as *Kajra re* and *Chhote-chhote shaharon se*
- *Determined youth*
- Youngsters who have run away from home

Event 2:

The movie, *Iqbal,* released in August 2005, was about a village boy, who is speech and hearing challenged, but a highly talented bowler and makes it to the Indian cricket team after determined and sustained efforts.

Depicted below is a gist of a mind map around *Iqbal*:

- High on talent
- Determination and dedication
- *Small-town* boy
- *High aspirations*
- Corruption in Indian cricket
- Strong support from the mother and sister for the boy
- *Against all odds*
- A mentor who believes in you

Event 3:

In Sept 2007, India won the T20 World Cup against all odds. The format was alien to the Indian cricket team back then. The team was a bunch of rookies (all the established players like Tendulkar, Dravid, Ganguly, Laxman had opted to rest) captained by an audacious young man named Mahendra Singh Dhoni, with hardly any experience of captaincy. The only player from Mumbai was Rohit Sharma, who never played in the 11 through the tournament.

Depicted below is a gist of a mind map around 'the T20 World Cup winning Indian team':

- *Youngsters*
- *Fearless* (inexperienced, hence no exposure to defeat)
- *Small-town* players

- *Wanting to prove themselves*
- Enthusiastic
- No hang-ups
- *Aggressive* captaincy
- *Risk-takers*
- Marriage between the sports and the entertainment industry.

Event 4:

The movie, *Jab We Met*, released in October 2007 was a huge hit, especially so in the hinterland of India (it grossed more in non-urban India than in urban India). It is the story of a starry-eyed, confident young girl from Bhatinda and a city-bred introverted boy.

Depicted below is a gist of a mind map around *Jab We Met*:

- A sardarni from Bhatinda
- *Small-town* girl
- *Devil-may-care attitude*
- *Run-away from home*
- Positive approach to life
- Follow your heart
- A girl getting a boy (who the parents don't know) home
- A prosperous agricultural family from small-town India

A simple analysis of these mind maps reveals a few common observations (marked in *italics* above): 'Youth from small-town India who want to make it big will not be intimidated by their supposedly superior metro-bred brethren and is willing to go the extra mile to make it big.'

Each of the above-mentioned events can be described as follows:

Bunti Aur Babli: The movie was all about the spirit of the youth of small-town India (Tier 3 towns, as marketeers would like to put it) itching to establish their identity and make a statement, 'We are not going to be left behind in the India growth story.' The fact that both the protagonists Bunty and Babli were shown to be crooks on the run, can be overlooked as granting a poetic license to the filmmaker. The fact that the movie became a top-grosser is a metric of acceptance of the spirit (that small-town India is establishing its identity) by the movie-going public of India. This is the same class that many businesses want to target.

Iqbal: The movie was about the determination of a hearing and speech challenged talented young boy from a village, who is a gifted cricketer. It was the story about how 'against all odds' the boy makes it to the Indian cricket team.

T20 World Cup: Circa September 2007, the 'Indian Cricket team won the inaugural T20 World Cup in South Africa'. A closer look at the composition of the Indian team reveals a strong tilt towards players from ... hold your breath ... Ranchi (Dhoni), Rae Bareli (R. P. Singh), Rohtak (Joginder Singh), Kochi (Sreesanth), Allahabad (Mohd. Kaif)....
More than 70 per cent of the players were from non-metros, up there with the best in the world ... actually, on top of the world. These kids were no longer intimidated by their counterparts from Mumbai, Bangalore, Chennai, etc. That was a long way from the 1980s and 1990s where a Kapil Dev was an exception rather than the rule. That was small-town India making its mark.

*Jab We Met***:** Released in October 2007, was a huge hit. Kareena Kapoor, playing the role of a chirpy sardarni from Bhatinda finally proved that she could act too. The family portrayed in the film was a prosperous agricultural family, albeit a conservative one. The film showed 'a girl getting a boy (not known to the parents) to her house in Bhatinda to stay over', something not quite seen even in urban India then. Kareena endeared herself to the movie-goers not just with her winsome charm but also her devil-may-care attitude: Mind you, it was all happening in Bhatinda, not in Mumbai or Delhi. The fact that the movie was a hit across the country (higher success in non-metro India) is a metric of acceptance by the general Indian movie-going public. This meant that 'the character of an independent girl with a mind of her own was accepted and empathized with by the supposedly "conservative" small-town Indian family'.

INSIGHTS

From the above-mentioned events, one can say that, back then, Tier 2 and Tier 3 towners were up there on the aspiration ladder along with urban India.

Let us take a typical profile that emerges from all the above-mentioned events:

'An 18- to 25-year-old who has a mind of her/his own and would like to demonstrate it.' Mind you, this is not seen as a rebel. This is a character that has been accepted by and empathized with by the supposedly 'conservative' small-town Indian families (as displayed by the popularity of these movies).

What does this profile mean for corporate India?

'In figures', let us focus only on the female population in this segment.

In India, in 2008 there were approximately 600 million youth in the age-group of 15–25 years. Assuming 80 per cent to be in the 18–25 years bracket, it was a whopping 480 million block. Considering that 48 per cent (male-female ratio was 48:52, back then) of these were girls, turned out to be an astounding 230 million. Coupled with rising female literacy, this was a potent combination.

What opportunities did this throw up for corporate India?

Newer markets for apparels, cosmetics, music and entertainment, etc. Does it stop at that? No, it doesn't.

What does an 'independent' 18–25-year-old girl aspire for?

1. A successful career

2. Freedom of choice

3. Financial independence

4. The ability to fend for herself

5. Standing out among peers

6. Glamour

7. Staying connected

Based on the above parameters, let me list down some predictions made based on this study back in 2008 and see what actually happened between 2009 and 2013.

Parameters	Predictions Made in 2008 for Non-Metro India	What Actually Happened in Non-Metro India from 2009 to 2013
Successful career, financial independence and glamor	• An air-hostess training academy could attract a lot of enrolment in Tier 2 and Tier 3 towns. • Training institutions for beauticians and spa staff, nutritionists, hospitality services. • IT training institutions would spread their presence. • A kind of 'finishing school' or a 'grooming academy' would also attract a good crowd.	• Frankfinn set up air hostess training centres pan-India in towns like Itanagar, Durgapur, Alwar, Palakkad, Thrissur, etc.[2] • A host of IT training institutes set up centres across India (NIIT/ APTECH/ etc.). • Salons and spas mushroomed all over small-town India.

(continued)

[2] https://www.frankfinn.com/training-program/

(continued)

Parameters	Predictions Made in 2008 for Non-Metro India	What Actually Happened in Non-Metro India from 2009 to 2013
Financial independence and being noticed among peers	Flaunting a 'credit card' is considered 'cool' in this age-group. However, if an 18- to 19-year-old girl was to have a credit card, it would invariably be an 'add-on'. She would be 'dependent' on her father or an elder sibling. After all, an add-on is not 'the real thing', is it? Should banks not look for some other metrics to judge the credit-worthiness of such youth.	Penetration of credit cards in rural India increased and the spending through credit cards increased by 29 per cent from 2008 to 2013.
Staying connected	Social networking sites would need laptops for access. How many electronic retailers have attempted to 'sell laptops in the Tier 3 town outlets'? Manufacturers of 'mobile phones with GPRS platforms' need 'to drop their prices' to become more accessible and widespread. These	• Croma (an Indian retail chain for consumer electronics and durables) had 101 stores across 25 cities and towns in India by 2011. • Mobile penetration in India rose in geometric proportions in that period.

Parameters	Predictions Made in 2008 for Non-Metro India	What Actually Happened in Non-Metro India from 2009 to 2013
	towns would lap it up. After all, it would cost a mere 25–30 per cent of what a laptop would.	• GPRS-enabled phones outsold other types in non-metro India.
Fending for oneself	Girls' hostels should increase in metros to tackle the influx of girl students into the cities.	The central government launched a scheme in the fiscal year 2009–2010 to construct multiple 100-bedded girls' hostels across the country.
Standing out among peers	Sports clubs could find a large following considering the achievements of many from amongst them.	A lot of sports, not just cricket, have generated a decent following across India. So many leagues have been launched for games which earlier no one cared to give a second look, for example, hockey, football, kabaddi, badminton, boxing, wrestling, etc.

TRY THIS!

Follow the five steps listed above in the chapter and plot the unique events in all the seven determinants listed for the next six months and become a trend spotter.

Chapter 9

Three-Dimensional Ethnography

WHAT IS ETHNOGRAPHY?

'Ethnography, in simple terms, is the study of cultures or a specific aspect of a culture. It helps understand the motivations of people's behaviour. Ethnographers spend long periods of time with the subjects they are studying, in their contexts. They often become a participant in the daily lives of their subjects. This enables the ethnographer understand the natural behaviour of the subject. Hence, qualitative researchers use various tools from an ethnographer's kit in their trade. Businesses, in their pursuit of understanding their consumers, have warmed to the discipline of ethnography. When ethnographic techniques merge with the understanding of psychology, it becomes a potent combination for a business wanting to fully understand its consumer. Remember the concept of 'last mile user connect', we spoke about earlier?'

BACKGROUND

Mahindra & Mahindra Financial Services Limited[1] is a rural non-banking financial corporation (NBFC), involved in the business of offering a wide range of financial products to address varied customer requirements such as housing, automobiles and other such assets. Their major market is rural India and the sales and operations teams

---

[1] Case study presented with permission of Mahindra & Mahindra Financial Services Ltd.

comprise 12,000 plus people who are in direct contact with customers and prospects. The profile of this team can be captured as follows:

1. They have their feet on the street at all times, that is, they travel continuously.

2. Their preferred language is their mother tongue, not English.

Mr Tushar Vaidya—General Manager, Learning & Development (L&D)—is responsible for training and developing these people to operate at maximum efficiency. He summarizes the challenges as:

1. 'Getting them together for a training program used to be a very difficult task. The sheer magnitude of people to be handled was logistically unmanageable and expensive. Moreover, every day that a field executive (handling operations such as sales, collections, etc.) is away from her/his territory translates into a revenue loss for the company.

2. There was no common language (English was not an option) that could be understood by the entire team. Even Hindi was not an option, since the company's operations spanned the southern part of India too, where Hindi is not spoken or understood very well. Hence, weaving together training programs for them was proving to be challenging for the L&D team.'

Till 2015, Tushar's team would organize classroom training programs region by region, zone by zone. In his words, 'My team would forever be busy organizing training programs. We would hardly get any time to assess the real learning needs of our field force.' Tushar added, 'We were intuitively feeling that something was amiss.'

1. The dropouts were high

2. The post-learning feedback was not very encouraging

3. Application of the learning was abysmal

4. We were spending heavily on these initiatives

'After every training session, my team would sit at the head office (HO) and analyse why the feedback was not positive. Team members would give their opinions on the same and problem-solving would happen on issues that we thought were the problems. Over a period of time, we realized that we were not solving the real problems and needed to know the learner more intimately. We needed to know the learner as a whole human being. Being a proponent of Design Thinking, I was inclined to use ethnography tools to do so. However, we had to build the capability (in our team) of carrying out an ethnography exercise.'

That's when Tushar approached DK with a brief that read, 'We need to know our learner as an individual, to be able to tailor our training modules and methodologies.'

Within a week, DK got back to him with a detailed plan about how he intended to go about this project. 'Each member of Tushar's team would be tagged to a field executive and would spend a week with him, shadowing him through the day and if possible, also spend time with the executive's family. This would enable the L&D team to understand the prospective learner in depth, his motivations, aspirations, complaints, peeves, frustrations in life, learning style etc.' (a detailed template of the observation diary is displayed further in this chapter).

When Tushar shared DK's plan with his team, there were a lot of reservations, such as:

1. We have sat through so many training programs till date and have gone through enough feedback forms in order to know exactly what our learner needs.

2. We interact with them so many times.

3. We have been in this company for almost eight years.

4. What new are we going to get to know?

5. Why such a rigorous process of shadowing and why throughout the day? We could do with an interview.

The team was not very enthused with DK's process. Tushar had to do a lot of convincing, it wasn't easy. But he didn't give up. According to Tushar, 'Unless they experience the process, they will not be convinced. The experience has to talk back to them.' Tushar's confidence in the process ensured that his team went ahead with the project (some willingly, some with reservations). He was ready to face the consequences, if it didn't go too well. He requested DK to conduct a training session for his team members on the proposed methodology.

DK's session included:

1. What to observe during the visits?

2. How to observe?

3. How to understand the functional and emotional needs?

4. How to understand the aspirations, motivations, likes, dislikes, learning styles, learning attitudes of the executives?

5. How to capture photographs/videos/audios? To understand and interpret body language, voice tone, etc.

The single most important communication to the L&D team was, 'We are not going into the field to solve a problem, but to understand the prospective learner from all perspectives and we must keep an open mind and pick up all clues.' The main purpose of this exercise was to understand the following:

1. Who our prospective learners are (in their environment)? What is their mindset?

2. What do they do? Why do they do it? How would they like to do it?

Now, have a look at the observation diary (attached at the end of this chapter) that DK had prepared for them.

Let's analyse and understand the contents of the same.

The Dos and Don'ts on page #1 are pretty much self-explanatory

UNDERSTANDING THE INDIVIDUAL: CONTEXT (PAGES 3 AND 4)

- Family background: people in the family, hierarchy in the family, decision-makers, educational qualifications, occupations.

- Aspirations: Family's expectations from the individual. The individual's expectations from her/his family members (younger siblings included). The individual's ambitions in life.

'*Why?*' A person's family influences the mental constitution of an individual. Hence, understanding the family's thought process is important (an individual, more often than not, works hard to live up to her/his family's expectations). His expectations from his younger siblings reflect whether he approves of his family's expectations from himself. If his expectations from his younger siblings are different from his family's expectations from himself, then, one can conclude that, that individual does not approve of the family's expectation off himself. This conformity or dissonance is the root of an individual's behavior and personality and hence his motivations in life. One can understand qualities and traits that appeal to an individual and knowing this is important to determine the learning style of an individual.

Significance for the L&D team: The underlying basis of content that one builds into the training methodology should, preferably, be in consonance with the traits and qualities that an individual approves of. If they aren't then the effectiveness of the training program is likely to go down.

DISSATISFACTIONS IN LIFE AND ATTITUDE TOWARDS THEM (PAGE 5)

- Dissatisfactions: What does the individual complain about in her/his own life? Is there a tendency to blame others/ circumstances for these?

'*Why?*' Dissatisfactions display discomfort with certain situations in life and hence they are actually manifestations of what a person wishes for but doesn't have. This lets us know his deep-rooted expectations in life.

Whether he has a tendency to blame others or circumstance helps us understand whether he takes responsibility of whatever happens or just passes the buck. This lets us know, whether he would take ownership of tasks, fight it out in a crisis or would rather blame others.

Significance for the L&D team: In the context of the learning process,

1. Would he be able to manage self-paced learning modules, or would he need constant supervision?

2. If an individual takes responsibility of whatever happens in his life, a project-based pedagogy would be better suited. For others, a more pedantic or a spoon-feeding approach might work better.

UNDERSTANDING THE INDIVIDUAL: PERSONAL DRIVERS AND LEARNING STYLE(S) (PAGE 6)

- Friend circle: how many close ones? How often do they meet?

'Why?' Close friends give away a lot about an individual—what values, traits, attitudes does the individual appreciate in life. Conversations with close friends are free flowing and many individual traits, biases, motivations come out during these.

Significance for the L&D team: If you are creating a story format for a training module, then the central character responsible for drawing out the learnings must display traits similar to those of the learner's friends. This would create an instant connect with the intended learner and hence lead to more engagement in the learning process.

- What activities do they do together?

'Why?' The activities that an individual gets involved in with his friends are some of the most liked ones.

Significance for the L&D team: This gives us information about how to keep a learner involved, by incorporating some of the activities that the learner finds engaging.

- Most favoured language (talking and writing) (Page 7)

This doesn't need any explanation when we are looking at creating a learning module

- Recreation habits? (Page 7)

- o Content viewing habits: regular/irregular? How much time? What types of programs does she/he watch? Favourite serials?
- o All-time favourite movies?

Significance for the L&D team: Content viewing habits give away preferred learning media. The kind of programs (content) that she/he watches gives us indicators of likes and dislikes. Favourite shows/movies are a clear indicator of what kind of plots/story lines excite the prospective learner. All this information can be used to enrich the content of the learning module to make it more engaging.

- • Favourite characters from:
  - o History
  - o Mythology
  - o Cartoons
  - o Movies watched

  For each of the above, ask why? (Page 7)

Favourite characters indicate what values/personality traits/ethics/ attitudes resonate with the prospective learner.

Significance for the L&D team: This helps craft the right kind of characters to be used in the training modules (story formats)

- • Information gathering platforms–how and where from? Newspaper/TV/internet. In the newspaper, which is the first page that she/he opens? (Page 8)

Significance for the L&D team: This is a no-brainer to get to know the media that the prospective learner likes and is most comfortable with.

Which page of the newspaper he opens first gives a fair indication of what he is most curious about?

Significance for the L&D team: This again helps us craft the contents of a training module around the learner's interests.

- • Political leanings (don't force, let it come out through a natural discussion)

One's political leanings give away an individual's deep-rooted expectations from society in general, which indicates a deeper aspect of the individual's thought process.

- Which were the favourite subjects in school/college? (Page 8)
- Which were the most hated subjects in school/college? (Page 8)
- Ask about favourite teachers from school/college. Probe why and what characteristics did they like about these people? (Page 9)
- Ask about the most hated teachers from school/college. Probe why and what characteristics did they dislike about these people? (Page 9)

Significance for the L&D team: Favourite/most hated subjects are clear indicators of motivators and demotivators in the learning process. Need I say more about the significance of knowing these while crafting a training module?

Favorite and most hated teachers are clear indicators of how the learning process/pedagogy should and should not be, respectively. If one wants to use an anchor character for creating an online module, what traits should the main character(s) portray, would be evident through this understanding.

- Which are the favourite games? Physical as well as online? How much time is spent on online games? (Try to assess why does the individual like the above-mentioned games).

Significance for the L&D team: Games are something that people play with total involvement; their hearts are into the act. Hence, they are an outright indicator of what challenges excite them, what metrics of performance people find interesting and also participate in without inhibitions. All this helps immensely in creating not just the learning content but also the evaluation rubric.

WHAT HAPPENED NEXT?

Equipped with the observation diary, Tushar's team went onto the field. For eight days, they got associated with field executives according to their linguistic backgrounds, for example, a Tamilian tagged along with an executive in Tamil Nadu, a Maharashtrian went into interior Maharashtra, an Andhraite tagged an executive in Andhra Pradesh, a Punjabi shadowed an executive in Punjab and so forth. The numbers were not large. DK and Tushar believed more on the quality of interaction rather than quantity.

Each member of Tushar's team spent the next eight days shadowing the field executives, right from the time she/he got out of the house in the morning. Shadowing means literally spending every moment observing what's happening without any interference. It means being objective and non-judgemental. The researcher has to be like a recorder and should observe things as they are, without the lens of self-bias. Staying non-judgemental is the most challenging and the most essential trait that a qualitative researcher must cultivate. As the team spent more time with the field executives, the observation diary began to get filled up with interesting observations. After a couple of days of accompanying the field executives, they became more friendly. Now, here's another red flag for a qualitative researcher, friendship, many a time, leads to loss of objectivity and the subject's behaviour gets interpreted through that lens, the researcher has to remind herself/himself about not losing objectivity.

Due to the comfort-level setting in, after the first two days, every member of Tushar's team got invited for dinner or breakfast at the respective field executive's home (DK had clear instructions about such things: No one would step into the subject's house without being invited. The reason being: the researcher should not be perceived as an intrusion. But if invited, the researcher should definitely accept it. Since that would give an opportunity to the researcher to spend time with the family and observe nuances of the subject's behaviour as well his social circumstances). During those eight days, most of Tushar's team members were invited for dinner or breakfast more than three/four times. Those were the kind of bonds that got developed—'one more red flag here'. Due to such bonds, the researchers got entry into the subject's close friend circle too without being perceived as an intrusion. The subject's interactions with her/his close friends revealed a lot of character traits that proved useful while crafting the content of the learning module.

At the end of every day, Tushar's team members would note the day's findings into the 'observation diary'. After the first few days, many dots began to get connected. All of Tushar's team members would exchange notes every night about their respective findings of the day. These conversations triggered off many a new line of enquiry for the next day. As the team got involved deeper into the research, they figured out some techniques on their own and experimented till they got them right.

RESULTS

Tushar says, 'My team members came back with multiple 'Aha' moments, they said, the real pain points of these people are not the same as what we thought they are, their lifestyles are quite different from what we used to think ... Now, we know our people much better and can visualize very different training content and methods (motivators, demotivators etc.).'

One of Tushar's team members (name not revealed to maintain confidentiality), spent 12 days shadowing executives in interior Maharashtra. She says, 'Initially, I was apprehensive about the process. I had doubts about whether the executives would accept us or not, whether I would be able to follow their routine? But as I began the exercise, I just eased into it. It was the first time that I was actually in their shoes. Earlier, our training programs used to focus on selling and collection skills, personal grooming etc. After this exposure, we realized that our field executives would be focused about the tasks assigned to them and were good at them. So we need not train them on operational skills such as selling/collections etc. We need to take advantage of their proximity to the customer. With this realization, we began to train them on cross-selling. Our field executives, many a time, are faced with daunting tasks such as dealing with emotional family members of a customer who is unable to pay his installment on time due to external circumstances. On the other hand, there were customers who threatened them with dire consequences if they came back to ask for unpaid installments. We had to train them to tackle such situations. Our inputs were also aimed towards raising their confidence and self-esteem.'

She goes on to say, 'The best outcome of this exercise was that I got to know my people so well that in any training program that I conduct now, I am able to use real grassroot-level examples. The audience connects with these examples very well and I have consistently received a feedback of 4.8 plus (out of five) for the training programs that I have conducted since then.'

Tushar corroborates, 'We never ever had that kind of intimacy with our field folks earlier. It was a very interesting and unique way of understanding our people. This exercise gave my team a very strong conviction about knowing our people. This conviction now enables us to take on not just L&D issues, but other HR matters as well. This is so much better than the statistical analysis that we would do, through feedback forms, prior to this exercise. Our methods of training, the content, even our budgets have changed drastically post this exercise. Back in 2017, we were much ahead of the curve in our industry, with our podcast-based training. We recrafted our content using story-telling with relevant characters that came out from the exercise. These characters were different in different regions of the country and were used parochially for the training content of executives belonging to that particular region.'

'One interesting insight that came out prominently was that our field executives are constantly on the move, on their motorbikes. They have a very strong bond of affection with their bikes. In our training content, the bike was used very prominently as a central character to drive home a lot of points—such as grooming, flawless after sales service for our customers, continuous contact with the customer, Customer Lifetime Value (CLV), etc. This made our content a lot more contextual and acceptable, rather than preachy and pedantic. That struck a strong chord with our audience who is a 22–24-year-old graduate from a mofussil town. They found the videos we created so interesting, that many went viral within their circles. The virality quotient, in fact, made our job much easier and the learning points that much stronger, since they came with a recommendation of their peers and not ours (the L&D team). Such videos, normally, have a short shelf life but these ones went around for almost a year and half. That ensured multiple views and hence stronger reinforcement of the learning points. The training was entirely self-propelled without any supervision from us. Isn't that how learning should happen?'

Tushar adds, 'Now, this process comes naturally to my team. It enables my team members to understand the core of the groups that they are in charge of.'

'Thinking back, when I connect the dots now, these learnings have laid the foundation for our future success of the learning pedagogies that we have created, for example, sometime back we tied up with Coursera for some of their online courses. Before signing up with them, we did a similar exercise with our people and shared the findings with Coursera and got the content and delivery methods curated accordingly. The communication strategy we used for promoting these modules internally was also driven by the findings of that exercise. The results have been amazing.' The following table depicts the effectiveness of our methodology against the industry average as well as Coursera's general success across their clients.

Parameter	Mahindra Finance	BFSI[b] Average	Coursera Average
Enrollment utilization rate	100%	68%	80%
Completion rate	67%	21%	40%
Learner Net Promoter Score (NPS)[a]	75	60	45
Learner rating	4.8	4.5	4.3

Source: Coursera for Business
Notes: [a] NPS: The likelihood of a participant to suggest the course to a colleague/peer.
[b] BFSI: Banking, Financial Sector, Insurance.

Tushar was recently invited to speak at a Coursera customer conference to share how they deployed their content at Mahindra Finance.

He concludes, 'The exercise which we did back then, forms the basis of every learning program that we launch now. Everyone talks the language of deep user understanding now. Earlier, we used to do a typical 'Training Needs Analysis', now we do a 'Complete Learner's Study' in the context of which the program is going to be delivered. The context then becomes the overarching theme. Because context is the most important thing today, even more important than content, since context precedes content. And that results in successful programs. Till 2015, our learning strategy used to be program content based. Now it is context based. We were way ahead in our industry, in introducing micro-learning as a strategy. Our pedagogy shifted towards delivering the learning points using contextual stories, humour and entertainment for our field executives. In a way, you have to compete for their attention, they have so many apps on their mobile phone. The observation diary has become a cornerstone for all our endeavors ever since. 'Knowing our Users' is the culture that has got ingrained in the organization and that has laid the foundation for our later successes.'

IMPRESSIVE IMPRESSIONS

Three-dimensional ethnography is not just another piece of jargon. Its application is not restricted to consumer-facing functions (such as marketing, sales and customer relationship management [CRM]). It can be used in every vertical/domain/walk of life, in a business/non-business situation.

1. Trying not to solve a problem but just attempting to know your customer. This attitude helps build a big repository of insights for future initiatives. This repository is the most valuable asset that an organization can build to make itself future-ready.

2. Trying not to solve a problem is not something many managers would attempt to do. Tushar Vaidya, in the above case was given the 'latitude to experiment. People such as

Tushar must be encouraged'. Organizations must encourage their people to experiment. CEOs and HR folks must change their attitude toward appraisal metrics and rethink these metrics (by giving importance to an employee's 'willingness to experiment').

3. Qualitative research is not rocket science. 'It is simple, but not easy.' That is an oxymoron, right? Why do I say that? Because the basic principles are really simple, but it is not easy to implement them:

   a. Remaining objective and non-judgemental—not easy at all.

   b. Recording things as they happen without bringing in your own bias into the ambit–not easy at all.

   c. Continuous observation and recording is not easy. One has to stay focused all the time. The initial feeling of fun often peters out as the research progresses. Hence, it is important to train the researcher really well. She/he should be good enough to experiment with some techniques on her/his own in the field to escape the boredom that may creep in.

   d. So train your research team really, really well.

To summarize, a manager wanting to know his customer has to:

   a. Be non-judgemental

   b. Be meticulous in observing everything

   c. Enjoy the process

   d. Experiment on the go, based on fresh insights

Observation Diary

Name of Subject:

Contact No:

Email Id:

Name of Field Researcher:

Contact No:

Email Id:

Dos and Don'ts

1. Spend as much time as you can with the subject

2. Establish their trust

3. Listen and be attentive

4. Notice subtle communication such as body language

5. Do not advise

6. Don't correct people, understand their perception

7. Participate in their natural habitat without interfering

8. Look for signs in the environment that might reveal behaviour, such as adaptability and compromise

9. Take pictures

10. Be sensitive about the cultural and social contexts

11. Look beyond what people say and understand what motivates their behaviour

12. Be respectful of people's values, their thoughts & feelings

13. Maintain an honest and open communication

Understanding the Individual: Context

The following information should be derived gradually and not asked for directly. Do audio-record these conversations, so that you don't get distracted while taking notes.

- Family background: People in the family, hierarchy in the family, decision-makers, educational qualifications, occupations.

_____
_____
_____
_____
_____
_____
_____
_____
_____
_____
_____
_____
_____
_____
_____
_____
_____
_____
_____
_____
_____
_____
_____
_____

Page 3

- Aspirations: Family's expectations from the individual. The individual's expectations from her/his family members (younger siblings included). The individual's ambitions in life.

_____
_____
_____
_____
_____
_____
_____
_____
_____
_____
_____
_____
_____
_____
_____
_____
_____
_____
_____
_____
_____
_____

Page 4

- Dissatisfaction: What does the individual complain about in her/his own life? Is there a tendency to blame others/circumstances for these?

_____

_____

_____

_____

_____

_____

_____

_____

_____

_____

_____

_____

_____

_____

_____

_____

_____

_____

_____

_____

_____

_____

_____

_____

Page 5

Understanding the Individual: Personal Drivers and Learning Style(s)

- Friend circle: How many close ones? How often do they meet? What activities do they do together?

_____
_____
_____
_____
_____
_____
_____
_____
_____
_____
_____
_____
_____
_____
_____
_____
_____
_____
_____
_____
_____

Page 6

The following information should be derived gradually and not asked for directly

- Most favoured language (talking and writing)

_____

_____

_____

_____

- Recreation habits?
    - Content viewing habits: regular/irregular? How much time? What types of programs does she/he watch? Favorite shows?
    - All-time favourite movies?

_____

_____

_____

_____

_____

_____

- Favourite characters from:
    - History
    - Mythology
    - Cartoons
    - Movies watched

For each of the above, ask why?

_____

_____

_____

_____

Page 7

- Information gathering platforms: How and where from? Newspaper/TV/internet. In the newspaper, which is the first page that she/he opens?

_____

_____

_____

_____

- Political leanings (don't force, let it come out through a natural discussion)

_____

_____

_____

_____

_____

_____

- Which were the favorite subjects in school/college?

_____

_____

_____

_____

_____

_____

- Which were the most hated subjects in school/college?

_____

_____

_____

_____

Page 8

- Ask about favourite teachers from school/college. Probe why? What characteristics did they like about these people?

_____

_____

_____

_____

_____

_____

- Ask about the most hated teachers from school/college. Probe why? What characteristics did they dislike about these people?

_____

_____

_____

_____

_____

_____

- Which are the favourite games? Physical as well as online? How much time is spent on online games? (Try to assess why does the individual like the above-mentioned games).

_____

_____

_____

_____

_____

_____

_____

_____

_____

_____

Page 9

It's Logical: Innovating Profitable Business Models

SECTION 3

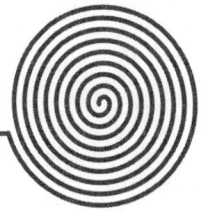

Let Your Consumer Define Your Business

Chapter 10

Hitting the Nail on the Head: What Does the User Seek from You?

In Section 2, we have looked at some interesting methods that can be deployed for user understanding. We talked about:

- How Sassy Vadapav understood the *real* choices and preference of consumers by making them play games.

- How an investment advisory could look at restructuring their offering by narrowing their research down to that one bull's-eye question.

- How a bank nailed the reasons for loss of customers using a simple observation methodology.

- How memetics could help companies anticipate trends.

- How a company restructured their entire executive training methodology by going beyond conventional user journey mapping.

- What immersive ethnography really means.

All these instances brought out the merits of specific methodologies in specific situations to hit the 'nail on the head', namely,

- Gamification of user research helps focus on understanding a consumer's 'real' choice.

- Getting to the bullseye question helped the investment advisory position its offerings the way their customer would want it to be.

- The bank example brought out how identifying that bullseye activity would nail a customer service issue.

Each of these are parts of the whole business strategy. Let us now look at how getting that 'bull's-eye' definition of a business helps craft a successful strategy. (Names of individuals and the company have been changed.)

In August 2012, Mr Sevakia, the founder promoter of Zen Jewels approached DK saying, 'DK, we have been manufacturing and exporting jewellery since 1992. Our clients include renowned merchant retailers like Swarovski, David Yurman, Buccellati etc. We have been recognized as their best supplier for the last eleven years in succession. We manufacture as per client specs but have absolutely no freedom of creative expression. Whenever we suggest any designs, our buyers shoot them down. And if any design is approved, it is an excruciatingly long and bureaucratic process .... Ours is an entirely B2B (business to business) operation. The customer who wears our products does not even know us .... we have absolutely no place in the mindspace of the woman who wears the jewellery that we so passionately create. Plus, we are at the lowest end of the value chain, with pretty low margins. The margins that these merchant retailers garner (on what we manufacture) are beyond astronomical, though I don't grudge them that. I am Sixty Nine (69) now, and I will be retiring in the next three odd years, but before that, I would like to create our own brand and leave a legacy for my sons. Businesswise, it makes more sense to promote a brand of our own (in addition to our B2B operations). If we have to double our topline in the next three years, we cannot be at the mercy of our merchant buyers. We *have* to create a brand of our own and sell directly to the end-user, i.e., I want to get into the B2C (business to consumer) space.'

MORE ABOUT ZEN JEWELS

Zen Jewels is a 100 per cent export oriented unit (EOU), operating out of one of India's export-processing zone (EPZ). They have three world-class manufacturing units in the EPZ. These units had been set up with technical help from the best consultants in the world.

The quality standards adhered to are better than most American or European manufacturers (Japanese manufacturers would probably give tough competition though). In 2012, the annual revenues were ₹3,620 million.

To summarize, the assignment was about creating a B2C brand owned by Zen Jewels and executing on the same by the end of financial year 2015.

THE INITIAL DISCUSSION

Sevakia and DK met at Zen's head office on 28 August 2012. With a cup of tea in his left hand, he gestured, 'So tell me your views about Zen.'

'Look Mr Sevakia, let us first understand what Zen has been doing all these years.' DK began, without beating around the bush.

'Yeah, 20 years, 3 months, 21 days and this morning.', clarified Sevakia, with a nostalgic look in his eyes. He was a tough individual, but that expression gave away the feeling that he was lost and seemed worried that Zen had hit the glass ceiling. He was happy with the way his sons were handling their responsibilities. But they were not dreamers, the way he was in his youth. Maybe it was the fact that, when he began his entrepreneurial journey, he had nothing to lose, while these kids were wary of making mistakes lest they be held responsible for what should be deemed a failure. It's the success of one generation that creates hindrances for the next one's ability to dream big and outimagine. Sevakia, realizing that his thoughts were drifting towards philosophy, turned to DK, with a nod, nudged himself to focus on the discussion.

Having somewhat realized what was going through Sevakia's mind, DK asked, 'So tell me what Zen has been doing for two decades?'

'What do you mean by what we have been doing for two decades? I have described to you, our entire journey: from setting up to where we are right now and what I want Zen to look like in the coming years.'

'Yes, but I would still like to know from you what Zen does,' DK prodded.

Sevakia's expression gave away a bit of anger as well as some intrigue.

DK continued, 'Yes, Mr Sevakia, what does Zen do?'

The same question being repeated was a bit much for Sevakia. He snapped back, 'We manufacture jewellery to the highest quality standards that exist, we supply to the most demanding brands in the world, who sell to the most demanding consumers in the world in the most demanding markets in the world. We have three world-class manufacturing facilities, set up with the help of top Japanese consultants. Our rejection rates are so low that our American and European competitors don't even mention theirs. We rarely miss our delivery schedules. Let me tell you, the last time we missed a shipment date was 26 months', with a slight pause, 'and five days back. Our processes are fine tuned to minimize scrap and we salvage 97.6 per cent of it. Only Takashima Jewelry of Japan could probably have a higher salvage rate. So **that's what we do**.' His expression was such that he would have thumped his desk hard, had it not been someone of DK's stature sitting in front.

'Wonderful Mr Sevakia, I already know about Zen's fantastic manu-facturing capabilities and believe me, I am in absolute awe of it, no two ways about that. But I would still repeat the same question, what Zen does? Or let me reframe it a bit, what business is Zen Jewels in?' 'And this time, try telling me in one sentence please, Mr Sevakia.', DK added.

Sevakia gave him an irritated look but he was willing to grant him the persistent probing, because deep within, based on DK's questions during their previous interaction, he felt that this individual had the ability to grasp the essence of things. And that he was onto something.

He responded, 'We manufacture world-class jewellery.'

After a pause, DK remarked, 'So you manufacture jewellery? That's what Zen does, but Mr Sevakia, that still does not answer what business Zen is in.'

'What?' Sevakia shouted, unable to mask his anger.

'Yes, Mr Sevakia, manufacturing jewellery is the operational part of your company, but it is not the business you are in,' there was a tone of authority in DK's voice.

'We manufacture jewellery, so we are **jewelers**.'

'That's what you sell, Mr Sevakia, every company sells what it makes.'

'So we are **world-class jewellery manufacturers who create world-class jewellery.**'

'Can you get a little macro, Mr Sevakia?'

By then, within himself, Sevakia had begun to think, 'Why did I even ask this guy to get involved in this project?'

The silence was broken by DK. With no change in his expression, he plodded further, 'Sir, tell me why does the end-user buy the jewellery that you manufacture?'

With a puzzled look, Sevakia retorted, 'To lay their hands on the best goddamn designs in the whole world.'

'Yes, but still, why does the lady wear the world-class jewellery that you manufacture?'

'**to look good** ... to show off,' grunted Sevakia.

'Ah! There you go, Sir. If the consumer of your jewellery buys it for **looking good, aren't you in the fashion business?**' DK quizzed, with his lips curled toward the right into a friendly half smile.

Sevakia stood there with the half-empty tea cup in his left hand, stunned. His thinking seemed to have stopped. His mind went blank. He felt as though a thunderbolt had hit the table separating the two of them and it was sizzling his brain. His eyes wide open, eyeballs locked into DK's. The walls of his office appeared to be crumbling, the entire office seemed to have disintegrated. Zen's factory looked as though it had imploded, rubble strewn all around and a cloud of dust rising up toward the sky.

Sevakia absent-mindedly slumped into his chair, his lips moved as though he were a robot and monotone emerged, 'Can we meet tomorrow?'

Trying to gather his thoughts, he managed to say, 'Let me think about this ...'

'Think about what?' DK enquired.

Shifting his gaze toward DK, from the Hussain that adorned the wall, he blinked a couple of times, 'Huh... ummm Yea, what you said sometime back ... what business we are in.'

The next morning, the meeting began with two cups of tea, brewed by Sevakia himself. This privilege was accorded to people he was intrigued by.

He began, 'Tell me what you mean by "We are in the **fashion** business?"'

'Look Mr Sevakia, what you make is immaterial. It's what your consumer seeks and gets out of what you make, is what is important. And that is what defines your business. So if a consumer buys your stuff to make herself look good, you **are** in the **fashion business**.'

Sevakia had pondered over it through the night and he was a lot more receptive. The morning yoga session, no doubt, had helped.

DK continued, 'So, Mr Sevakia, now if Zen Jewels has to expand and you want to create a brand of your own, the first question I would like you to answer is, Who is the consumer you are targeting?'

Assuming some crypticness in the question, Sevakia did not respond.

'Sir, who do you want to target with the new offering that you want to create?'

After the previous day's experience, he was reticent. DK repeated the question, 'The business has to start with someone willing to buy your stuff, right? So who would you target?'

'Look, in all these years that we have been exporting jewellery, we have realized that the segment that buys our jewellery is the working lady in the 28–37-year bracket, in North America, Western Europe and Australia.'

'Are you sure Sir?'

'About this, I am absolutely certain. I have had very long chats, over the years, with all our merchant buyers, I have visited their show-rooms innumerable times, have been a party to meetings between our design teams and their procurement teams. That category of consumers has always been the focus. We know that segment the best. The entire promotion by all our buyers is targeted toward that segment.'

'One more question, Sir. How have been your sales over the last three years? Can I get to see the actual numbers, if you don't mind?'

Sevakia opened his laptop and displayed a spreadsheet.

'These are the revenue numbers. Can I see the unit volumes?' asked NK.

'Let me call Rafiq,' said Sevakia.

Leaning towards his speakerphone, he instructed, 'Amita, please ask Rafiq to come in with his laptop asap.'

Rafiq, a portly gent, in his mid-forties, with a deeply furrowed forehead that gave away the years spent trying to balance balance sheets. He was a chartered accountant and headed the management information system (MIS) at Zen.

Asking him to sit, Sevakia directed Rafiq, 'Please share the numbers for the last three fiscals, value and volume, both.'

After a few clicks on the keypad, Rafiq turned the laptop screen towards Sevakia.

'Rafiq, please show it to him.'

DK looked at the spreadsheet for a few moments, thanked Rafiq and turned towards Sevakia, and summarized, 'The topline has grown no doubt, but the number of units sold has almost plateaued. The revenue growth has come from price increases. In fact, for some product categories, unit volumes have degrown.'

Sevakia responded, 'Yes, that's what is worrying me …. Do you need anything more from Rafiq?'

'No'

'Rafiq, thanks. I will call you if we need anything more.'

After a longish pause, DK said, 'We should study this 28–37-year-old western working woman.'

'The unit volume in that segment has degrown, we should look at other women,' Sevakia objected.

'Before we abandon that segment, let us understand the reasons why that is happening.' Retorted DK and added, 'Let us commission some research in those geographies. I know some friends who can help us out.'

During the next meeting, DK began, 'Do you agree that Zen Jewels is not in the business of manufacturing jewellery, but in the business of fashion?'

'Yes, but …'

DK cut him off, '… and you are actually losing customers and we need to find why?'

'Yes'

'So my research question is, 'How do these 28–37-year-old working women consume fashion in those markets?'

'Can you clarify please?', enquired Sevakia.

'The question intends to find two things, namely

1. What does 'fashion' mean to this woman?

2. Where does she buy what she means by 'fashion'?'

'Tell me if what I have understood is correct' Sevakia wanted to be sure,

1. 'What products comprise her definition of 'fashion'?

2. Where does she buy these products from? Right?'

'Yes'

'What else will you ask the researchers to find out?'

'Nothing' responded DK

'That's it?', Sevakia had a bewildered look on his face. 'How long do you think it will take?'

'I am afraid, nothing less than eight to ten weeks'

'That's too long.'

'Sir, all I can say is that, 'Rome wasn't built in a day.' DK smiled back.

The research began in the same week. The brief to the research team was simple.

After multiple skypes and conference calls between DK and the research team, the report was ready. During those 10 odd weeks, Sevakia did get fidgety but to his credit, he did not try to short circuit the process.

In mid-November, just after Diwali, the festival of lights, DK and Sevakia sat to analyse the report. DK shared the findings and his insights in detail. He had read through the report four times to crystallize the contents and glean out the essence.

'Mr Sevakia, let's keep this simple, the research shows:

1. What does fashion mean to our target consumer?

    a. Luxury handbags

    b. Fragrances

    c. Glamorous apparel

    d. Cosmetics

    e. Jewellery (not necessarily high end)'

'So what's new?', interjected Sevakia, 'We knew this three months back too', obviously he was irritated.

'Hold it Sir, there's more to come …', without getting distracted, DK continued,

    a. 'High-end mobile phones

    b. Frequent visits to Fine Dines,

    c. A game of golf with her female colleagues,

    d. Getaways to exotic destinations and so on

also form a large part of her 'fashion' spend'

Sevakia's jaw dropped with the expanding list. The rest of what DK presented was a blur. He had grasped the significance of what DK was saying but wasn't able to connect with how Zen would use these insights.

Sensing Sevakia's impatience to connect the dots, DK, narrowed his eyebrows and continued, 'Our study highlights that 43 per cent of the above items were purchased **online** by our target consumer (the 28–37-year-old working western lady).'

There was a long silence, as Sevakia tried to put the pieces together. Finally, his patience got the better of him, 'So?', he raised his baritone, wanting DK to spell out his strategy.

'Sir, we have absolutely no presence online, we must create it'

'Eh … no one buys jewellery online' scoffed Sevakia.

'I have that covered, Sir. When the research team shared this predominance of online shopping behaviour, midway through the study, I asked them to check 'What's the maximum ticket size our target consumer (TG) would be comfortable swiping her card, for an online purchase'? The team's findings suggest that our TG is not comfortable swiping a credit card for more than $490 for an online transaction. I have corroborated this number with Google's analytics too. So if we go online, then….' DK paused to look straight into Sevakia's eyes to gauge his reaction to what he was about to say.

'To go online', DK reiterated, 'We **cannot continue** with our existing range of $1,200 to $1,500 varieties. **We will have to create a whole new portfolio in the $350–$500 range.**'

By now, Sevakia was upright in his seat. Combatively, he retorted, 'Do you even know what it takes to redesign an entire portfolio of jewellery? It is **not** like introducing a new spring or winter collection by some apparel brand. They just have to cut and stitch patches of different fabric together. **We will have to recreate all our molds on the investment casting line.** Do you know what that would mean in terms of time and effort? I am not even mentioning about the other changes in the production process.'

'Yes Sir, I do know. But would you **rather make what might sell or try to sell what you make?**'

DK continued, 'Trying to sell what they make is what most companies do and finally they hit a wall. But companies that constantly find out what consumers want and then make that, are the ones who make it big. They are the ones who keep reinventing themselves based on trends and almost always are **future-ready**. You have to decide what Zen has to do.'

The operational manager in Sevakia was more comfortable with 'Selling what you make'. But the visionary entrepreneur within him resonated with the 'Making what might sell' bit.

It took some time and more arguments, for him to be convinced about the visionary entrepreneur's approach.

After another round of tea and biscuits, he queried, 'So we shouldn't have any brick-and-mortar presence, huh?'

'No Sir, that's not what I meant.' DK continued, 'We need to look at it holistically. Let us look closely at what I said earlier. Our TG frequently visits Fine Dines, golf clubs and the like. Why not bring these places on our sales map? We should have sampling inventory with product catalogs at such places and train the *maitré d'*, etc., to speak about and describe our designs ...'

'You expect these places to stock our stuff?', demanded Sevakia.

'No sir, just samples. Orders should be taken online, but on the spot. So we have to create a tech ecosystem that enables booking of orders at these places. Deliveries could happen later, the same way they are done by e-tailers. This way, we can increase our visibility among the target group without having to increase inventories at outlets. That will free up cash flow too.'

DK continued with an air of finality. 'Pure-play brick-and-mortar retailing also needs to be relooked at. Our stores should not be located in any of these Gold Souks. We should have our presence next to.... Say an iStore or a Louis Vuitton and the like because **we need to be present where our TG shops for fashion** ... think about it.'

That hit Sevakia like a thunderbolt, 'Moving out of Gold Souks and being present where the TG shops for fashion.' That statement found a strong resonance with the visionary entrepreneur within Sevakia. The conflict within had ended.

Dk continued, 'To understand and execute on these new sales channels, we need people who have experience in those domains, that is, we need to rope in people from there to set up our operations.'

(Over the next four months, Zen recruited the then sales head of India operations of Rolex. They also poached the Asia-Pacific operations head from Zara. These people added tremendous value in setting up the new sales channels)

Over the next few months, Sevakia led a no-holds-barred taskforce to create an entirely new product line to be marketed under the 'Zen' brand. It took them a little under seven months to create the product line, put an entire backend in place for online selling, appoint retailers as suggested by DK. Besides the strategizing and planning, DK was involved in getting things done. By June 2013, the 'Zen' brand of jewellery was in the market.

CIRCA APRIL 2017

Zen Jewels had hit a topline of ₹8,320 million (up from ₹3,620 million in 2012), 41 per cent of which came from Zen brand of jewellery, that is, the branded jewellery line that was launched in June 2013 had grown from zero to ₹3,410 million by April 2017. Interestingly, 61 per cent (₹2,080 million) of this came from purely online sales. Remember someone had said, back in 2012, 'Nobody buys good jewellery online.' Be that as it may. Moreover, latest analysis of the consumer profile shows that younger women too have been buying the Zen brand of jewellery. So now they have expanded their consumer base.

The earlier line of business (B2B selling to Swarovski, David Yurman etc.), had grown from ₹3,620 million in 2012 to ₹4,910 million in 2017. If you calculate the year-on-year growth for the B2B business, it had actually degrown if you take into account inflation from 2012 to 2017.

Once again, the business model innovation trumped technological innovation and was easier to execute. Disclaimer once more: I am not saying one is better than the other.

IMPRESSIVE IMPRESSIONS

Defining what business you are in should begin with the consumer, what she/he gets or seeks out of what you offer. Unfortunately, most corporations define their business from the perspective of their own capabilities. More often than not, that restricts them from riding the next wave of business. Let us understand with a few examples:

Let me ask you a question, 'what would be PVR's competition?' (PVR, as you all know is a chain of multiplexes that screen movies.)

Most would say, other multiplexes, single screen theatres. The lateral thinkers amongst you would add television, Netflix, Amazon Prime, TataSky, Torrent, etc.

Now, let me reframe my question, 'Imagine it's a Saturday evening and you have had a rough week, all you have in mind right now, is too have a good time. What would you do?'

- Go out for dinner
- Go pub-hopping with friends
- Enjoy a good set of tennis with buddies
- Go to a gaming zone
- Retail therapy (go shopping)
- Go for a movie
- Catch a stand-up comedy show
- Watch a good play at a nearby theatre
- Book a turf and have a good game of football
- Go over to a friend's place
- Call friends over

- Read a nice book
- Maybe, go for a long drive with dear ones
- Just sleep at home

I am sure, you have already thought of a lot more.

Now, look at the above list and notice that 'Go for a movie' is just one of the many options that you have on a Saturday evening. So my question is, **'Are other multiplexes, single screen theatres, tv, Netflix, Amazon Prime, TataSky, Torrent**, etc. the only competitors of PVR?'.

All the answers to my 'Saturday evening' question are modes of 'having a good time' on a Saturday evening, so **are they not PVR's competition too?** Should PVR not look at those avenues for diversification?

Of course yes, because all of them take the prospective consumer's disposable spend away from PVR, and 'any option that PVR's prospective consumer spends money on, instead of on PVR, is PVR's competition.'

What do the other modes actually do for the consumer? 'They help her/him have a good time. So can we not define PVR's business as **helping people have a good time**?' The moment you define it like this, a whole bunch of avenues open up for PVR to expand its business. These ideas come to mind only when you look at your business from the perspective of your consumer, what she gets/seeks out of what you offer. That precisely is a consumer-centric approach to business.

- Was Kodak in the business of photography? **No, it was in the business of helping people relive their memories.** Had they understood it, they would have championed their own digital cameras rather than trying to defend their photo film business.

- When Kellogg's came to India in 1994, were they in the business of breakfast cereals? NO, they should have defined their business as **being in the breakfast business**. Had they defined it that way, they would have bothered to find what Indians had for breakfast instead of trying to change the breakfast habits of Indians. They would have been better off spending, possibly, ₹600–800 million in 1994 on setting up a modern plant manufacturing ready-to-eat Poha, Upma, Parathas and the like. Mavalli Tiffin Rooms (MTR) captured that position and was extremely successful. Kellogg's in India, on the other hand, spent hundreds of crores of rupees on advertising, trying to change Indian breakfast habits and are still struggling.

Let us look at the growth of Google in its first decade of existence (1998–2008):

If I ask what Google's core business was, most would say, it was a 'search engine' or an 'advertising platform'. I disagree, I would say that Google's main business, back then was 'satisfying human curiosity'. Search engine and advertising platforms are what they did to support the business of 'satisfying human curiosity'.

Let me ask you a simple question, 'Why do you visit www.google.com?' Obviously to look for some information. But why do you need information? If you dig further, you will realize that humans seek information because they are inherently a **curious** species.

Google understood this and built a gigantic business around this simple truth. By virtue of the search platform that Google runs, they have access to what people are looking for, in absolute real time, that is, they know what people are **curious** about in absolute real time. In its first decade of operations, it just kept acquiring content creators that provided people with content that they were curious about:

- When they realized that people were looking for directions from place A to place B, they went and bought over 'keyhole', the company that specialized in providing that content. Keyhole was the genesis of the immensely successful 'Google Maps'.

- When Google realized that people were exchanging photographs on a platform called Picasa, they went and bought out Picassa web albums.

- When Google realized people were interested in sharing videos on Youtube, they went and bought Youtube and the rest is history.

- When Google realized that people were trying to get in touch with long-lost friends on a platform called Orkut, they did not try to create another Orkut, they just went and bought Orkut.

There will be many more, some unsuccessful ones too. That did not pan out the way they had thought it would. Nonetheless, that didn't deter them from pursuing a sound policy, based on a very deep understanding of 'what business they were in'.

Whatever people were curious about, Google acquired or forged strong synergies with content creators who created that content and figured out ways to monetize these acquisitions. By themselves, these acquired companies had virtually no revenue models. Google created the monetizing strategies.

Fundamentally, Google capitalized on **human curiosity**.

The Concept of Core Competence Hampers Strategic Thinking

If you look at the future only from the lens of what we are capable of (core competence), then that's a very myopic way of looking at business. But if you look at what is emerging, what consumers are seeking and answer the following questions:

1. How can we restructure to tackle the new market needs?

2. How can we reskill our people to ride the upcoming trends?

3. How can we shift to a new normal?

4. How can we be nimble enough to change gears depending upon the changing consumer expectations?

5. How can we adopt emerging technologies?

It's Logical: Innovating Profitable Business Models

Time to Pick Your Brain

1. Suggest some diversification avenues for the following companies:

    a. ESPN

    b. NIKE

    c. Apple

    d. Paytm

    e. Airtel

    f. Shoppers Stop

    g. Life Insurance Corporation of India (LIC)

    h. State Bank of India (SBI)

    i. Infosys

    For stimulating ideas and discussion on the above, connect with my team.

2. Think about what business your company is in? (Remember DK's advice to Sevakia, 'not more than one sentence')

    _____

3. Who are the competitors to your business? (no word restrictions here)

    I.   _____

    II.   _____

    III. _____

    IV.   _____

    V.   _____

    VI.   _____

    VII. _____

    VIII. _____

    IX.   _____

X. _____

XI. _____

XII. _____

XIII. _____

XIV. _____

XV. _____

XVI. _____

The more the merrier!

SECTION 4

Decoding the Neural Networks of an Innovator

Chapter 11

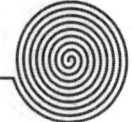

About DK

In July 2001, DK was sitting at his desk at Precision Automation Systems Pvt Ltd (henceforth referred to as PAS, the company he founded in 1990). He was peering into a spreadsheet depicting the company's performance over the previous six years (1995–2000 and the first quarter of 2001). The big worry in his head was, 'Where will growth come from in the next three years?' Competition was duplicating PAS' designs and selling cheaper.

ABOUT PAS

PAS was an engineering company located in Mumbai, that had begun operations by manufacturing different types of presses. These presses would be used for performing some core operations such as riveting, punching holes, marking logos/serial numbers, bending small metal strips, crimping of terminals onto wires, etc. Such operations are most prevalent on the manufacturing assembly lines of automotive components, switchgear components, utensils, toys, stationary items such as files, etc. Over the years, PAS had developed a fairly comprehensive range of table-mounted presses suitable for these operations. In addition to these standard presses (SPs), PAS had developed various modular automation devices (MADs) used on assembly lines. Under the MADs range, there were products such as modular indexing tables (turntables with controllable movements), linear motion control devices, miniature pick and place units, automatic feeders for rivets, screws, etc.

Up to 1998, SPs and MADs accounted for most of PAS' revenue. PAS' fairly successful transition from a company manufacturing basic SPs to reasonably sophisticated MADs and custom-made SPMs

(Special Purpose Machines) was the result of a combination of factors: DK's keen understanding of customer requirements, willingness to work closely with them, strong urge to experiment with different modules (he would spend hours on the assembly lines of his customers observing every operation in the manufacturing process, many a time, himself working along with operators for shifts at a stretch to understand the intricacies of the various processes involved).

A BIT ABOUT DK, THE INDIVIDUAL

As a student, DK possessed a rebellious streak under a seemingly calm exterior. Declining a fancy offer from a global petrochemical giant, during the campus placement at his alma mater (Jamnalal Bajaj Institute of Management Studies, also referred to as JBIMS), during his MBA (1988–1990) and venturing out on his entrepreneurial journey was a matter of immense pride for him. He has a BTech in electrical engineering from IT BHU (now rechristened as IIT Varanasi). DK once confessed, 'By the third semester of my BTech course, I had lost all interest in engineering and had toyed with idea of dropping out to pursue a career in copy writing and story-telling at an advertising agency. But then, somewhere toward the middle of the fourth semester, Professor Subba Rao (who taught us Non-linear programming) tickled my fancy for technology. Professor Rao inspired me to get serious about my studies and my grades which used to be in the lower quartile of the class, began surging up.'

At PAS, in 1996, when he created his first special purpose machine (SPM) for an electrical relay manufacturer, he had thoroughly enjoyed the process of conceiving a unique idea and bringing it to reality. He had found his calling in life. After successful installation of that SPM at the customer's factory, he got an order for three similar machines. He was on cloud nine. That order was executed swiftly, which gave him the confidence to approach another relay manufacturer. He had thought it would be a cake-walk, thinking that this manufacturer would immediately place an order for at least one unit. But the purchase manager asked, 'Where can we see a similar machine in operation?' DK had no answer to this: he could not take this manager to a competitor's factory to show his creation in operation. Such information was confidential and never shared. Back in the 1990s, the World Wide Web was not so widespread. To counter this, DK did the obvious. He began to click pictures of every new SPM that PAS created, printed flyers with these pictures and elaborate descriptions of how those machines could multiply the output of an assembly line. But then prospective customers still asked, 'Where can we see the machine in operation?' It was definitely a very logical question. The photograph was a static image and customers would not bet a relatively large sum on something that they had not seen in operation. DK slept over this for a few days and came up with a solution 'Henceforth, I will shoot videos of every new SPM that we make before dispatch and show these video cassettes (back in 1996, CDs were just about getting known as a memory device and USB sticks did not exist) to prospects'.

So then, video cassettes replaced the printed flyers in his sales kit. On his next sales call, very triumphantly, he took out the video cassette only to be told that there was no video cassette player in the office. DK offered to let the prospect keep the video cassette so that one of the decision-makers would carry it home and watch it on the family video cassette player (VCP). DK called back the next day and asked expectantly, 'How do you feel our machine works?' In other words, 'Don't you think what you saw on video is great and will enhance productivity on your assembly line?' From the other side of the line, he got a matter-of-factly response, 'Oh! The video cassette…I forgot to carry it home yesterday, can you call back tomorrow?' DK would dutifully call back the next day to get a reply, 'Oh! I reached home very late, so…….' The day after that he got a response, 'Oh! There was this serial running last night and the family had monopolized the television set, so could not watch the video' (back then, households used to have only one television set).

Over the next few months, DK realized that the cost of making these videos, getting them edited professionally, etc., was only enhancing his knowledge of the TV viewing habits of his prospects. **He had to figure out a way to show a demo during his first sales call**

itself (remember, there were no laptops then and even desktops were a rarity on a work desk).

On a vacation to Mahabaleshwar, a hill station about 250 km from Mumbai, that year with family, a cousin was showing off his Sharp viewcam–a bulky, 2 kg video camera with an in-built screen and a video playback facility. By the end of the four-day vacation, DK had figured out an answer to his question, 'How to show a demo of his SPMs in the first sales call itself?'.

On his return to Mumbai, he bought a Panasonic viewcam (that was cheaper than the Sharp model), shot his SPMs in operation and began to run the playback videos across the table, to his prospects. From the facial expressions, he could see that people across the table liked what they saw and were willing to talk further.

With a little push, they placed an order. This trend continued. PAS' sales conversion ratio increased.

The Sales Push: The newly found demo tool was showing encouraging results. Naturally, DK thought, 'All my sales agents must have a viewcam'. The catch was, back then, a Panasonic viewcam cost a whopping ₹45,000 and he would need ten of them (by 1996, DK had appointed nine sales agents across the country). The total outlay would be close to half a million rupees. A resource-constrained, growing company did not have that kind of reserves. So DK went to PAS' bankers, asking for a term loan to finance the purchase of ten Panasonic viewcams. The manager at the bank, on receiving the application was dumbstruck, 'DK, you want half a million for giving a fancy home entertainment gadget to your sales agents'? However, convinced DK was about the investment, no one around was willing to finance it. He finally sold some of his family hirelings to raise about ₹0.3 million (would be about ₹3.3 million in 2019) , scrambled the rest from his savings and borrowings from close friends. By Aug 1996, all of his nine sales agents were proud owners of a Panasonic viewcam. Sale of SPMs and MADs showed an aggressive upward curve in the ensuing months. DK's investment in the 'fancy home entertainment gadget' was paying off.

By 1999, MADs and SPMs had overtaken the standard presses in their contribution to the total revenue. SPMs were clearly emerging as the stars of the margin game. Every SPM was a new challenge that DK revelled in.

Professionalizing: Towards the end of 1996, DK had roped in Mr Harish Kumar (henceforth referred to as Harish), to look after the marketing function at PAS. Harish brought along close to 10 years of experience in industrial marketing with his stints in a couple of multinational distribution houses dealing in engineering goods. By Jan 1998, Harish had set up a good Pan-India network of sales agents (of course, each of them was equipped with a viewcam: by then, prices of these viewcams had dropped by 50%).

The understanding between DK and Harish worked well, allowing DK to focus on his passion of designing newer MADs and SPMs. Between 1997 and 1999, DK designed 16 different types of SPMs. PAS seemed poised to launch itself in the next orbit. Though, to begin with, DK had dithered over letting go off his control over marketing by roping in Harish: After all, DK had founded and built PAS on his own toil and sweat. He had put his personal life on hold, delaying having a baby for five years into his marriage to his college sweetheart. He had clocked 15 hour days consistently from 1990 to 1996 building PAS into a small yet highly responsive organization. Everyone in PAS came to him for advice on all kinds of decisions.

Though not a control freak, DK enjoyed the feeling of being perceived as intellectually superior. Harish, with his professional grounding in multinational companies, was more of a process-driven decision-maker and demanded his space for independent decision-making. Initially, DK construed Harish's independent streak as a threat to the control that he himself had over the operations of PAS. However, he was aware of his own limitations as a marketing person (for DK, a customer asking for a discount was like a slap on the face, that demeaned the effort put into creating a new design). Letting go off control over a part of PAS' operations was a tough thing for DK. It took about six months for DK, after inducting Harish, to come to terms with the new power equations in the organization and let

Harish take over independent control of the sales and marketing function.

In October 1997, DK offered a 15 per cent stake to Harish. Today, DK confesses, 'Giving up control was not a rationally arrived at decision, it was more out of not being able to say no to various requests from Harish to let him get on with his aggressive customer acquisition tactics. In hindsight, I can say that it worked out well, but I had definitely lost sleep for a few months back then.'

All through 2000–2001, the Indian manufacturing sector was showing signs of growth and that made DK feel buoyant about the future of PAS.

Sales were going upward, however, competition was heating up. Two of them, namely Axial Systems Pvt Ltd. (henceforth referred to as ASPL) and Convergence Automation (henceforth referred to as CA) were catching up a lot of ground behind PAS. Customers were cozying up to the lower pricing and easier payment terms of both ASPL and CA. SPMs supplied by PAS were being taken apart at customers' factories and reverse engineered by ASPL and CA, sometimes at outrageously low prices. PAS was losing out on repeat purchases.

In July 2001, DK was peering into his desktop and what he saw was not very pleasant.

Revenue from SPMs was dropping, sales agents of PAS were being forced to compete on pricing and easier credit terms. DK had strong reasons to believe that PAS' sales agents in Delhi, Ludhiana and Hyderabad had been entertaining enquiries from ASPL and CA and were giving away old leads.

ASPL and CA were getting in and cloning PAS' designs really cheap. DK foresaw many more players getting into this space in the near future.

A few things, however, were not that straightforward for the cloners, for example:

- Certain machining processes that led to accurate assembly fits of the various components of the SPM could not be figured out by mere visual inspection. To figure that out, it called for an in-depth understanding of machine design and manufacturing processes.

- Thorough understanding of the metallurgy of components used.

- Detailed market information with customer profiles and their exact requirements.

The cloner would have to necessarily spend considerable time and effort in reverse engineering and also identifying the right customers. Reverse engineering involved understanding the accuracies of machining, the process of machining, the metallurgy of components, the optimization of the control system, components and sourcing.

Thus, cloning involved quite a bit of trial and error. Many a time, unsuccessful trial and error at the customer's cost would lead to the cloner getting blacklisted as a vendor and that is always a big risk.

Typically, a clone[1] would appear in the market after PAS had sold about 10 to 15 units of one type of an SPM. This used to be the typical lead time that a clone would need to overcome teething troubles and this period would either make or break the cloner's foray into that sector.

For a first mover such as PAS, the initial 10–15 units would be the ones that would churn out the highest profitability. During this period, PAS would also gather good understanding of the entire target sector in terms of:

- The number of players in that sector

- Installed capacities of the various players and hence the potential for similar SPMs in that sector

- The geographical spread of the various players

---

[1] Patent laws in India were practically non-existent for this industry. All the hard work put in by DK would bring forth little return after the initial spurt of 10–15 deals.

- The different influencers in the sourcing process in that sector
- The scope for slightly tweaked versions of the basic SPM

DK needed answers to the following questions:

1. Where would the next phase of growth come from?
2. Should PAS continue manufacturing SPMs despite diminishing margins?

Chapter 12

DK's Dilemma

Conventional logic dictated that PAS shut down the SPM division and focus on standard presses and MADs to ensure consistent growth. SPMs consumed too much designing effort without a consistent return.

After many a sleepless night, DK asked Harish a few fundamental questions, 'What's our core competence? Is it not designing new stuff? So why should we be bothered about maintaining market share once all these clones enter the fray? Should we not keep moving to the next level/market?

Harish interjected, 'What exactly do you mean by the next market?'

DK replied, 'We design new stuff, command our price initially and then are left compromising on margins once these clones enter. Just think about the time and energy we spend on maintaining turf that's quickly shifting away from our strength. We cannot continue this way. Here's what I think: Let us focus on our core strength of designing. As of now, we come up with around 4–5 new SPM designs every year. Let me add a few good design engineers to our rolls and churn out double the number.'

Harish was left dumbfounded by his CEO's fanciful thoughts, he thought, 'Is this guy in his senses? We are losing money on SPMs and here's this nutcase talking about spending more money on a sinking ship.'

DK, oblivious to Harish's internal reasoning, continued with his plan, 'Look, these cloners, ASPL and CA spend considerable time and effort figuring out what we have designed. They do manage to reverse-engineer our stuff but in the process, at times, they do goof up and lose customers. What if we offered them our refined designs and ask for a fixed plus variable royalty? We could give them all the details of the design with a commitment that we won't manufacture the same SPM again. We could offer them the following:

- All design blueprints
- All machining and assembly standard operating procedures (SOPs)
- All metallurgical specifications
- All sourcing details
- All market details that we gather during our initial foray
- Access to our sales network

Think about the time and manhours we could free up and focus on what PAS does best: 'Imagining and designing new machines.'

Harish interrupted. 'But why would they pay us if they can clone, though with a bit of discomfort?'

DK replied, 'I have no solid response to this question right now. But in my gut, I feel that ASPL would be open to something like this. I would want to broach this with them to begin with.'

By the end of October 2001, DK had inked a deal with ASPL, though with a few modifications to his earlier musings. The deal read 'ASPL shall pay a consolidated down payment for every SPM design, the value of which shall be determined on a case-to-case basis. In addition, ASPL shall pay a royalty of 5 per cent to PAS for every SPM sold using the said design. After sales service shall be provided by PAS for an initial period of three months after every such agreement……. (other details included the information to be passed on from PAS to ASPL about market details, access to PAS' sales network etc.).

By June 2002, the agreement had begun to prove beneficial to both PAS and ASPL. DK expanded his design team, got more time to automate new processes and create new applications. ASPL got quicker and assured entry into the market without loss of face due to uninformed trial and error.

By December 2002, CA too had been roped into the collaborative initiative.

With all this going on, Harish, the marketing head and second in command at PAS had initially felt that he would become dispensable in the bargain, since the needs of a marketing and sales structure were becoming irrelevant at PAS. DK had to do a lot of convincing that generating market info to be passed on to ASPL and CA, as a part of the agreement, was as significant as sharing the design details. Over a period of time, Harish discovered that anticipating market size and strategizing was more exciting than managing and monitoring weekly sales. This stimulated him intellectually and was far more fulfilling than managing operations and the occasional excitement of appointing a new sales agent.

DK had been simultaneously working on shifting the manufacturing capabilities of PAS from their own shop floor to those of ASPL and CA.

Since 1996, DK had consciously attempted to analyse processes on the shop floor to determine which were critical and which were not, which needed to be done in-house and which could be outsourced. By 2000, he had managed to raise the percentage of outsourced components to 62 per cent. By mid-2002, this figure stood at 93 per cent. All this was done without retrenching a single employee. The methodology adopted was a simple two-step logic:

1. Any process that had to be outsourced, would involve the set of concerned machines to be disposed of. The operators working on these machines were offered the option to start off on their own using these machines. They would have to arrange their own premises. PAS would ensure minimum monthly orders. PAS would supply the raw material and guarantee a processing fee (decided with mutual consent). For a period of 18 months, PAS would ensure assured business to them, after which they would be free to look

for other clients and the guaranteed fee would reduce proportionately. Many operators got together and opted for this scheme.

2. Any operator who did not have the necessary skills to choose the abovementioned option would be trained and reskilled for other activities. Due to increased outsourcing, quality assurance had become crucial, so such workers were trained to become quality inspectors at various vendor sites.

With these policies in place, by mid-2003, only that machinery remained on PAS' shop floor, which was required for prototyping and trials. Moreover, PAS gained indirect control over the shop floors of ASPL and CA. The freed-up shop floor at PAS amounted to about 65 per cent of the real estate that PAS owned. DK liquidated it and turned it into an investible cash surplus to fund PAS' design and development initiative.

DK used a sizeable part of this cash to buy 25 per cent and 32 per cent equity stakes in ASPL and CA respectively, while maintaining entire control over PAS. This arrangement served a dual purpose:

• Making much needed cash available to ASPL and CA

• Reaffirming DK's commitment to the joint venture

By the end of 2003, PAS had gotten to be known as a design and development hub in its operating domain. DK could now focus entirely on his passion and Harish could concentrate on market sizing and identifying opportunities and let DK do the rest.

In 2005, the collaborative triumvirate of erstwhile competitors (PAS, ASPL and CA) was awarded a state government recognition as 'the most innovative company in the machine tool sector' in the small and medium-sized enterprises (SME) category.

Later that year, DK cashed out to an external investor at an undisclosed personal valuation.

IMPRESSIVE IMPRESSIONS

Let us dissect what DK did back then. Did he really innovate on the product? Did he innovate with some fancy technologies? A resounding '**no**' for both the questions.

This is a classic case of 'business model innovation'. Let us analyse further:

1. DK's constant focus was on the 'operating model' and after identifying his operational costs, he was constantly asking the following questions:

   a. **Which of these costs can be reduced or eliminated completely?**

      Relentless focus on this question was the key behind his running a lean manufacturing outfit. Due to this focus, he was able to reduce costs and add value simultaneously.

      Because of this, he was able to free up a lot of PAS' real estate, which he liquidated to acquire sizeable stakes in his competitors. A highly uncommon phenomenon in the SME space. I want to emphasize once more that DK's laser-sharp focus on the above question helped him execute this 'creative financial restructuring' of three competing business entities.

   b. **Which of these costs should be increased in line with the planned strategy?**

      When he crystallized his strategy of PAS becoming a design and development hub, he upped his spend by recruiting seasoned design engineers instead of cutting costs. It paid off within a year by doubling the number of new designs being developed.

2. DK's obsession with 'creating win–win situations' and the ability to successfully execute on it.

a. With his outsourcing strategy, the machine operators on PAS' shop floor were getting redundant. Did he retrench them? No, he actually created entrepreneurial opportunities for them by encouraging them to start off on their own. By offering them a guaranteed order flow for 18 months, he was able to assuage their apprehensions about the uncertainties of entrepreneurship.

   Do you think that this was philanthropy? Obviously not, if he had retrenched his machine operators, they would probably have joined his competitors (who would have been more than eager to absorb them considering the insider information they would bring along). Some of the operators might have become competitors for PAS, who knows?

   This was clearly not philanthropy; I would rather term it as 'enlightened self-interest'.[1]

   Those operators who did not opt for this offer, were retrained and reskilled as 'quality inspectors' for PAS' increasingly outsourced model of manufacturing. 'Nobody lost their jobs (another win–win)'

b. By investing in his competitors, he was able to leverage on everyone's strengths:

   i. PAS' strength of machine design

   ii. ASPL's and CA's strength in manufacturing.

   Their combined front enabled them to achieve a lot more than what they individually could have. A classic case of 'sum of the whole being much more than the sum of the parts'.

---

[1] Enlightened self-interest is a philosophy in ethics which states that persons who act to further the interests of others (or the interests of the group or groups to which they belong), ultimately serve their own self-interest (source: https://en.wikipedia.org/wiki/Enlightened_self-interest).

Once again, DK's penchant for 'creating win-win situations' shines through.

What would have happened if DK had not initiated this collaboration?

All three (PAS, ASPL and CA) would have competed, bled each other and died a slow death within the next few years. Once again, it highlights DK's attitude of 'enlightened self-interest'.

Multiple Perspectives

Unfortunately, our education system does not teach us this concept that would enable us to create win-win situations in life.

We have been brought up on an overdose of 'killing competition', haven't we?

To simplify and automate evaluation, our examinations are based on 'multiple choice questions (MCQs)'. A surfeit of MCQs has made us believe that a problem has only one solution. Through this, we are embedding binary thinking into young minds, that is, something is either wrong or right. This instills a thought process that I term as 'this or that', whereas life is all about 'this and that'. Our education system does not encourage a student to appreciate multiple perspectives to the same problem. We need to imbibe that ability to encourage creative problem solving and hence create more innovators for the future.

DK summarizes this entire initiative by saying, 'If I hadn't done this, somebody else would have. I was only the one who initiated the events, and everybody else joined in. and ends it with, 'The future is **collaboration**. Knowledge is omnipresent, so are competencies, we only have to figure out creative ways to come together and create arrangements where no one loses.'

This sums up DK's ability to visualize win-win situations and bring them to reality.

SECTION 5

Thinking Tools for the Business Innovator

Chapter 13

Scouring the Nooks and Crannies in the Ecosystem

So far, we have discussed various business model innovations and the rationale behind each of them. Do these ideas come as a flash or is there some groundwork that people like DK are involved in. How do they condition their brains to keep it so simple and yet churn out something innovative?

Don't you think all that DK has told us is simple? At the end of each one of DK's stories, did you not get the feeling, 'Ah! That was so simple, why did I not think about it earlier?'

According to me, that is the beauty of a truly innovative concept. **It is simple!!!**

Now, let us try to get a peek into DK's brain and how it churns out an endless stream of **simple** yet **innovative** concepts.

I asked DK, 'What is the groundwork that you do which creates the fertile soil for idea-gems to bloom?'

DK is a shy individual. He squirmed in his seat, felt uncomfortable handling direct praise, blurted out, 'Hey, firstly by referring to those simple concepts as idea-gems, you are elevating them to too high a pedestal. It's nothing that complicated.'

'Please enlighten me', I insisted.

After a bit of cajoling, DK relented, 'Whenever, anyone approaches me with a problem statement, the first thing I do is to take a chart paper and create a canvas of all the stakeholders involved in the ecosystem. It takes a bit of time to do that. Then I park it aside, that is, I don't really look hard at it.'

Puzzled, I asked, 'You just said it takes a bit of time to do it and then in the same breath, you say that you don't look at it too hard, I'm confused.'

'Yes, I don't really look at it much then', he added. 'I just keep it on my table or pin it to a soft board next to my desk through the duration of the project.'

This was getting intriguing.

Sensing my confusion, DK continued, 'Let me explain with an example. A couple of years back, I was involved in a project with the municipal corporation of our city. The aim of the project was as broad as, 'To create better pavements in the city'. Let me recount that for you.'

Looking at me in the eye, DK hurled a question at me, 'You tell me who are the stakeholders of a pavement?'

Surprised, I replied, 'The people who use the pavement ... Pedestrians, who else?'

Not impressed by my response, with a mischievous smile, DK quizzed, 'Who else? You tell me, I asked you the question.'

He went on, 'What about the contractors who are responsible for the construction and maintenance of the pavements? Should they not be considered as stakeholders? How about the urban planners?'

I interjected, 'But these are not beneficiaries from the pavement, hence not stakeholders.'

DK explained, 'According to me a stakeholder is any entity that affects the final design of the product or service that one is creating. That's my definition of a stakeholder and if you want to create a great product or a service, then you need to identify all of them. You may not satisfy all of them, but you need to be aware of them. You never know how you may need to connect with them in order to create a successful solution.'

He continued, 'How about the public utilities such as the telecom service providers, the water supply network, the power supply companies? Don't their cables pass under the pavement, so should their needs not be taken into account while designing a pavement? For maintenance purposes, the easiest access to the cable and pipe network is the pavement, so we must make proper provisions for the same through the pavement.'

'Two-wheelers: These are not supposed to be parked on the pavement, right? So those barricades need to be embedded on the pavement to prevent them from climbing onto it.'

'Four-wheelers: Have you noticed, sometimes when we park our cars by the edge of the pavement and open the door of the vehicle, it grazes the surface of the pavement or gets stuck in there. Why does that happen? The ground clearance of automobiles all around the world has a standard measurement. So, should the height of the pavement too not follow some protocol?

'Street-vendors?' I resented this, 'They are encroachers and a nuisance to the pedestrians. How can you consider them to be a stakeholder of the pavement?'

DK responded, 'Look, some of them, if not all, do have a valid municipal license and are present on the pavement by right, not as encroachers. Imagine if there were no street vendors, you would probably have to travel a couple of kilometers to the nearest store for buying a few lemons. These vendors do ease up our lives. Imagine if tomorrow a ban were to be enforced on them and they were asked to vacate, all of them would be out on the streets protesting, bringing the city to a halt. Can the administration afford this confrontation? So we need to design our pavements in such a way that some of them (not all) can be accommodated.'

'Shop-owners lining the pavement. Their requirements need to be considered too.'

'Residential buildings whose gates open onto the pavement. We often find kids playing in the compounds of buildings. Imagine a kid on roller skates, comes out of the gate at full throttle. Shouldn't there be a barricade that prevents her/him from falling onto a road with cars running at high speed. Where should such a barricade be placed? On the pavement, right? This scenario has to be taken into account while designing a pavement, or not? Hence, isn't such a building a part of the stakeholder ecosystem of the pavement?

'Signage that one sees on the road: Their positions are extremely important for road safety, directions and other such requirements. These banners have to be properly located on the pavement. That's something that needs to be thought of while designing a pavement. A standard pavement design cannot be replicated across the city. Different localities need different signages and hence an adaptable pavement design.'

'Traffic signals: The position of a traffic signal is non-comprisable; hence the pavement has to be properly designed around it. The power cables for the traffic signal will have to be laid below the pavement and they will need maintenance from time to time, so there should be a proper duct built into the pavement to facilitate the same.'

'But these are not living beings, how can they be considered as stakeholders?', I protested.

A little irritated, DK confronted me, 'Who says non-living entities cannot be stakeholders. Remember my definition of a stakeholder. Any entity that affects my final design has to be considered a stakeholder. Because if I don't, then my solution will never be holistic.'

Without waiting for my response, he continued,

'Junctions of crossroads: Crossroads determine the location of traffic signals; they affect the pavement design and hence are a stakeholder.'

DK was classifying everything under the sun as a stakeholder of the pavement.

Sarcastically, I asked, 'So aren't trees and animals too stakeholders of the pavement?'

He gave me that familiar look, which meant: hold your judgement and listen, smiled and continued, 'You are getting a hang of what I am saying.

Trees form an important part of the pavement's ecosystem; can you uproot a tree because you want to construct a pavement? No, the local municipality will not allow you to. So you have to build the

Figure 13.1. The Protector Ring around a Tree

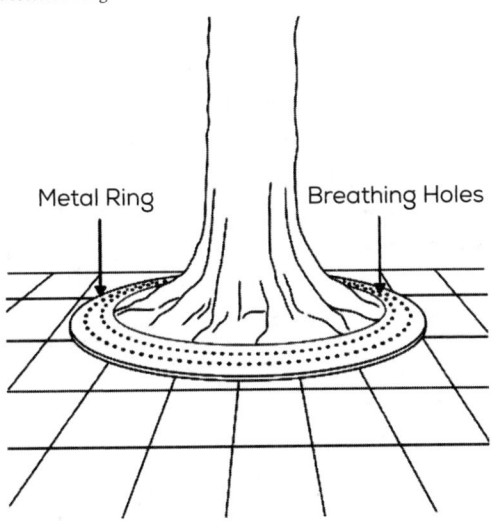

Metal Ring   Breathing Holes

pavement around the tree. Look outside the window and look around those trees on the pavement. What do you see? The roots of those trees are jutting out from the sides and have broken some of the tiles. To avoid that, a well-designed pavement must have those circular metal plates (as shown in Figure 13.1) around the tree so that the root system gets pressed down and does not protrude out from the sides.'

With that piercing gaze and disarming smile, both rolled into one, he asked, 'You said animals too, right? That's a brilliant point. In our country, you will find not just cats and dogs on the street, but cattle too. If you go to Rajasthan, you may find camels too. In some towns, you will find monkeys too.'

'But you cannot make things comfortable for them, they should not be on the pavement', I objected.

Shrugging aside my objection, he continued, 'I am not saying the pavement should be designed for the animal's comfort. I agree that animals should not be moving around on the pavement. But in our country they do. Can you cull them? No, you can't. You have to co-exist peacefully. You have to acknowledge their existence and

Figure 13.2. Gaps within Paver Blocks

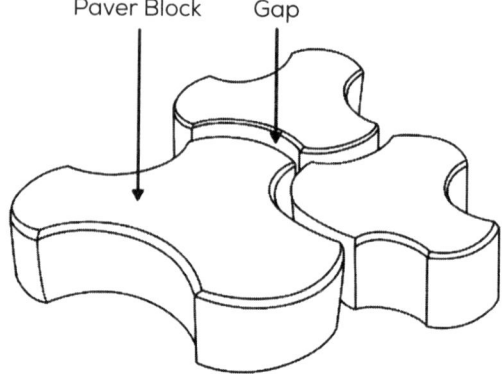

Paver Block   Gap

hence create a pavement with that consideration. Look wherever, these animals go, they pass their motions, they don't ask us whether it is ok to do so or not. Does that not affect us, the taxpayer? Who cleans up after that? It is the municipality staff that does the job of cleaning up. Now, most of our pavements are made of those jigsaw-like paver blocks (Figure 13.2).

Look closely at those blocks, there is a sizeable gap between adjacent blocks. All the animal poop stuck in these gaps cannot be cleaned up, however much the cleaners try to. So is this not a problem? Should the gap in these paver blocks not be reduced or removed completely. Do you still feel animals don't affect the design of a pavement?'

I could not refute this logic.

DK went on, 'Homeless folks who make the pavement their homes.'

'But they are not supposed to be there, and they do not pay taxes', I resisted.

'Agreed they do not pay taxes, but can you ignore their existence on the pavement? There is some littering where such folks live. It causes discomfort for you when you pass such areas. But have you ever paused and thought why this happens? They do not litter on purpose; they do not have access to basic sanitation. So, if I were the in-charge of 'pavement design' of this city, I would actually commission a survey to study the density of such populations around the city and pass that information to NGOs such as *Sulabh Shauchalaya* and ask them to construct sanitation facilities at the appropriate locations. Would the littering not reduce, if not stop completely? And these facilities will have to be built by the sides of roads along the pavement. Where will the water supply and plumbing to these come from? From under the pavement, right? So would the presence of homeless folks not affect the pavement design?'

'Garbage bins and garbage collection trucks: Garbage bins have to be placed at designated locations along the pavement and care should be taken that these positions should be such that they are easily accessible to the garbage collection trucks. The trucks have those hydraulic mechanisms to pick up the bins, tilt and empty them. All this has to happen smoothly, but don't you find at many places, the bins are placed in a corner which is not accessible to the truck. You also must have noticed the struggle that the municipality staff have to go through while emptying such bins. Moreover, a lot of trash spills onto the area around, never to be picked up. Hence, proper locations have to earmarked for the bins on the pavement.'

'Drainage gutters: A gutter is meant for water to pass through in case of flooding. So the pavement around a gutter must have a gradual gradient, so that water flows into it. If there's no gradient, then water would accumulate causing flooding. The insignificant gutter affects the pavement design.'

'Bus stops: On narrow streets, buses stop on the road slowing down traffic, sometimes causing jams. There should be a bay which ensures that the buses don't obstruct traffic when they halt at designated bus stops. The bay should be a part of the pavement design.'

'Foot-over bridges and subway entrances: Where do these open onto? On the pavement. So, don't they affect its design?'

'When you said pedestrians, did you treat pedestrians as one block?'

A little confused, I responded, 'Yes'.

He continued, 'Aren't there different types of pedestrians? Some on wheelchairs, some visually challenged, some with crutches and so on. Should the pavement design not take their requirements into account? Ever seen a young mother pushing a perambulator (pram) with her baby in it, trying to cross a road at a junction, in any Indian city? What does she do? At the junction, she picks up the pram from the pavement places it on the road, pushes it along, crosses the road, picks up the pram again, places it on the opposite pavement and then pushes it again. Inconvenient isn't it? Shouldn't the pavement have a comfortable slope at least at junctions to avoid inconvenience to such folks. A wheelchair bound person too would appreciate it.'

'At these new metro stations, about 14–15 inches from the edge of the platform, there are these yellow-coloured tiles that have embossed circles on them. What are these tiles meant for? They are referred to as 'braille tiles'. A visually challenged person walking along the platform with her/his walking stick can feel these tiles and gets to know that she/he is approaching the edge of the platform and should stop immediately. Should such tiles not be embedded near the edge of the pavements, at least at junctions?'

Smiling from ear to ear, he repeated his earlier question, 'Should pedestrians be treated as one block?' I was looking for a place to hide.

He looked at me and said, 'If we continue this analysis for another 10 minutes, we can list another 25 stakeholders, what say?'

Not waiting for my response, he continued, 'Will you answer two questions honestly?'

Still trying to find some chinks in his logic, I croaked, 'Yes'

'Question number one: Initially, how many stakeholders had you thought a pavement would have?'

Embarrassed, I responded, 'Not more than three to four'.

'Now, question number two: We spent quite a bit of time listing down the stakeholders of a pavement, was this a wasted exercise in the context of our quest of designing a better pavement?'

How could I refute his flawless logic?

DK continued, 'Listing out the stakeholders (as shown in Figure 13.3) at the beginning of a problem-solving exercise helps me understand

Figure 13.3. Stakeholder Map for a Pavement

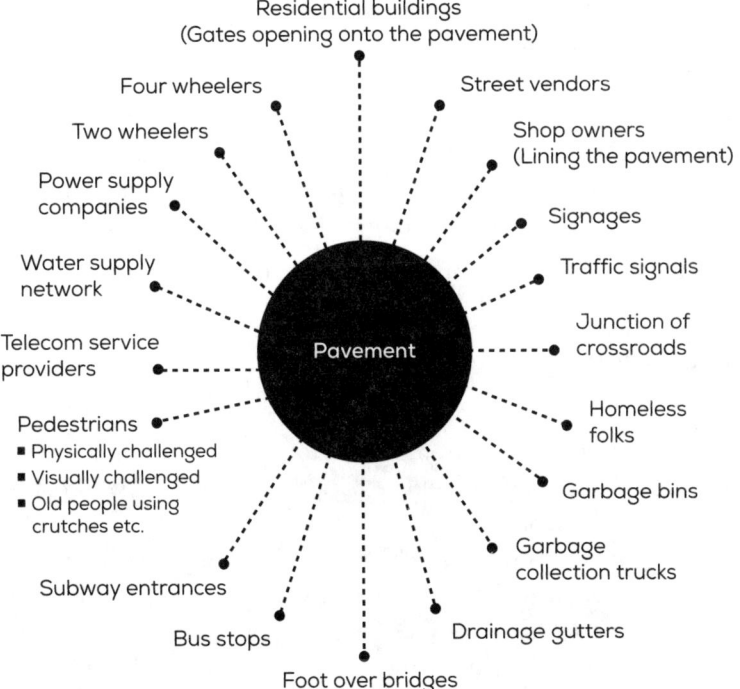

Stakeholder map of pavement

Residential buildings
(Gates opening onto the pavement)

Four wheelers

Two wheelers

Power supply companies

Water supply network

Telecom service providers

Pavement

Street vendors

Shop owners
(Lining the pavement)

Signages

Traffic signals

Junction of crossroads

Homeless folks

Pedestrians
- Physically challenged
- Visually challenged
- Old people using crutches etc.

Garbage bins

Garbage collection trucks

Subway entrances

Bus stops

Foot over bridges

Drainage gutters

the ecosystem better. It helps me identify the interconnections between them and that proves useful when I look to create *win-win situations* that remain sustainable.'

I queried, 'What do you do with this stakeholder map? Do you constantly keep analysing it?'

'No, as I mentioned earlier, once I make it, I don't consciously look at it, I keep it spread on my desk or pin it onto a soft board close by, throughout the period of the project. Occasionally, as I think of more stakeholders, I keep on adding to the chart. The chart gives me a macro view of the entire ecosystem in which I am trying to solve the problem. When I am relatively free and dozing off at my desk, I keep looking at it and that helps me find some non-obvious connections that prove handy, while executing on the business model … for that matter, even while executing on non-business issues.'

"My main focus is on how these varied entities in the ecosystem can be brought onto a common ground, where everyone benefits from each other's core strengths. That takes time to figure out. But once those synergistic areas are found, then it is not difficult to convince them. Even if everyone doesn't join in at the beginning, there are always these fence sitters. But after a while, when they see those on the playground benefitting, they jump in too.'

'It's not that difficult as you make it out to be', he concluded.

IMPRESSIVE IMPRESSIONS

1. Envisaging the ecosystem at the outset, while solving a problem, lays a strong foundation for things to follow. It helps in opening up multiple perspectives to the same problem. One appreciates the need/role of different stakeholders in the ecosystem. This helps in creating solutions where coordination between multiple agencies is essential. When one looks at an issue from the point of view of different stakeholders, the chances of creating **win-win solutions** get tremendously enhanced.

2. Normally, when we solve problems, we consider three or four stakeholders that are obviously visible. However, when you systematically map the ecosystem as shown above, multiple stakeholders get uncovered. Their issues get highlighted due to which the problem definition, more often than not, changes drastically, that is, the **real** problems get visibility. When this happens at the beginning of the problem-solving exercise, one would obviously avoid situations where one ends up solving something completely different from what the users seek to be addressed.

3. Thus, in-depth stakeholder mapping ensures good product-market fits.

It's Logical: Innovating Profitable Business Models

Chapter 14

A Cheat Sheet to New Product Creation

So far, we have discussed various methods of pre-research before getting into the ideation phase. All of it is absolutely necessary and cannot be short-circuited. However, sometimes innovators/managers are running short on time. What happens when there's a deadline to meet and your team feels there's not enough time to conduct elaborate user research?

There are many new product development (commonly referred to as NPD) frameworks. Some focus on manufacturing and production, some on the process to be followed, some on marketing and perception. However, I haven't come across any that addresses the issue holistically. In this chapter, we will explore an easy-to-apply, comprehensive framework[1] for the same. This framework (refer to Figure 14.1) can be used for creating breakthrough products and services, for innovating on processes as well as on organizational design. It is as useful for startups as it is for large conglomerates.

It is a sort of cheat sheet for creating innovative products and services.

The framework is an outcome of more than a decade's experience of working through various new product/service creation projects. It comprises around 73 attributes that people value in a product or service. This list is an ever-growing one, since after every project a few attributes get added.

---

[1] This chapter has been adapted from the article available at: https://link.springer.com/article/10.1186/s13731–016–0055–7

Figure 14.1. Universal New Product/Service Creation Framework

If you are short of time and want to jumpstart the solution generation process, this framework is a great starting point. Look at each attribute and see whether it applies to the product/service that you are trying to create. Of course, the relevance and importance of each attribute have to be checked from the users' perspective, not yours.

Not all of these attributes would be applicable to a product or service. Determining which ones to be incorporated calls for deep user understanding and research.

Let us look at some of these attributes, what they mean and how you can use some of them in the next product/service that you are going to launch.

Convergence to multiple modes or interoperability: Nowadays, we get these universal serial bus (USB) on-the-go (OTG) sticks which have a sliding mechanism. If you slide it towards one side, a USB port comes out while if you slide on the other side an android port comes. This enables the USB stick to be used on a laptop as well as on an android phone, that is, it can be used on multiple media.

OR

A website whose interface is dynamically formatted such that it fits on the large screen of a laptop as well as the small one of a mobile phone or the medium-sized one of a tablet. Such a website format is convergent to multiple modes.

Modularity: A product is said to be 'modular' when it consists of standardized units or sections for easy construction. This allows the end-user to create multiple options using the same basic building blocks, for example, Lego. In a service offering, there could be different features which could be added or deleted to enhance the user experience. Addition or deletion of any feature(s), in this case, does not affect the performance of the core offering, for example, the recently launched variable tariff option by Tata Sky (direct to home services), wherein a user can add/delete channels that she wants to watch.

Comfort: The level of comfort the product offers to the user. How comfortable is it to use the product? To enhance the comfort level of a product, 'ergonomics' is a vital characteristic.

> **Ergonomics:** Ergonomics[2] is an applied science, concerned with designing and arranging things that people use so that the people and things interact most efficiently and safely. It entails the study of the dimensions of the human body, in order to create products that can be used comfortably and efficiently. Hence, it fits under the umbrella of 'comfort'.
>
> This is easy to visualize for a product. Is it applicable to services? Yes, it is. If you were creating a website or an app, it would be helpful to know the angle at which people hold the mobile phone in their hands. This determines the angle which their eyes form with the surface of the device (i.e. the angle of incidence with the eye level). This angle would determine the location of the relevant callout buttons to be placed on the screen. It would also affect the choice of the colours used for these buttons, since colours

---

[2] Merriam-Webster dictionary.

Figure 14.2. The Learning Curves

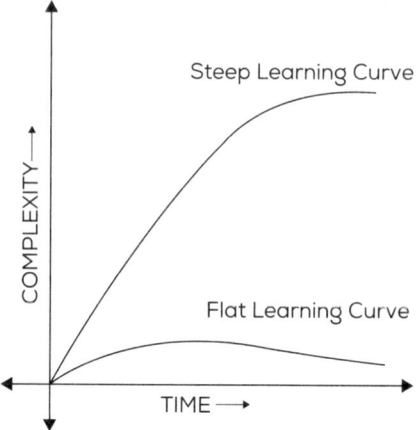

look different from different angles. Hence, if you want to design an easy to use and desirable interface for your app, you better understand the science of ergonomics.

Flattening the learning curve (Figure 14.2): When a product is so designed that the learning phase for using the same is very short, for example, an old-fashioned bottle with a lid, the moment one looks at it, one realizes how to use it. One does not have to read an instruction manual to understand how to use it.

The digital dial of the iPod is a classic case in point. The user did not find the need to be trained to use it. That leads me to the next attribute.

Intuitiveness: The interface should be so intuitive and uncomplicated that usage should flow naturally.

Non-verbal communication: Does the product communicate to you without you having to read the instructions about how to use it. This is an extension of intuitiveness of the product/service.

Traceability: If you lose your USB stick, how easy is to find it? Tough, right? All of them look the same. You can't differentiate between USB sticks of the same brand unless you have your name engraved on it, can you? There's no 'traceability'. However, if you lose your smartphone, the 'Find My Phone' app helps you trace its location. Your smartphone is 'traceable'.

Another way of understanding traceability is: in case, a car user complains about problems due to manufacturing defects, the chassis number of your car helps the manufacturer trace the car to its batch/ lot/date of manufacturing. This is very handy in case call-backs or replacements are mandated. The barcode or the QR code on the snack food that you buy, serves the same function.

Bundling of accessories: When a product is available together with the necessary accessories, for example, people would prefer a mobile phone that had an in-built charger, as against the conventional charger that one has to carry separately and which one forgets many a time. A built-in charger would avoid those inconvenient experiences. If relevant accessories are bundled with a product/service, the user experience becomes that much more seamless and pleasant.

Customized dosage: Patients who suffer from high levels of blood sugar (diabetes) require regular shots of insulin. There are devices such as the NovoPen that help inject insulin into the body at a click of the cap, just like a ball-point pen. No matter, how hard or how lightly you press the cap, the device can be programmed to inject exactly the pre-scribed amount of insulin into the body. The device has a customizable setting for patients who require different doses of insulin as per their blood sugar levels, body weight and other such parameters, that is, 'the dosage can be customized' as per every individual's requirement.

Poke-yoke (Japanese for mistake-proofing): Try inserting a USB into the USB port of your computer while doing something else, there's a 50 per cent chance that you will end up forcing it in the wrong way.

OR

Try inserting a high-definition multimedia interface/ video graphics array (HDMI/VGA) connector into your laptop, chances of getting it right are once again 50–50. The USB port and the connectors in question above are not mistake proofed, that is, they do not account for the mistake the user might make while using the product.

On the other hand, the pin of the iPhone's charger can be inserted into the phone both ways, the same can be said about the latest C-pin of the charger of OnePlus phones. Both, the iPhone charger and the OnePlus chargers **are** 'mistake proofed'. It reduces/eliminates user irritation with your product. User irritation is the prime obstacle to product adoption. People remember irritants more strongly than they remember pleasant experiences. Hence, user irritants **have** to be eliminated. If you can't eliminate them at least try hard to reduce them.

Self-correcting: The 'autocorrect' functionality on our smartphones corrects our spelling mistakes, that is, the software has the ability to self-correct.

Restrictiveness: if you are a left-handed person, try using a standard pair of scissors? Not easy, right? The product is restrictive. Why should it be so?

Inclusiveness too falls under this category. Does the product ensure social/gender equality?

Responsiveness: How quickly or easily does the product respond to the user's commands? For example, how quickly or easily does your car respond to the press on the accelerator pedal or how you can take a turn using a finger on the steering wheel?

Transparency of user feedback: The rating facility on the Uber app, whereby you can rate the quality of the ride (driver's courtesy, car condition, etc.). The driver too can rate you as a passenger. Both these ratings are visible on the app, that's 'transparency of user feedback'. eBay introduced this system long back (one could rate the vendor on service quality), to ensure reliable vendor performance.

Turn-around-time (TAT): The time taken between two successive occasions of usage of a product/service. Suppose you shut down your laptop, how much time does it take to restart the next time you put it on? A couple of minutes is what it takes for the system to restart. The TAT, in this case, would be two minutes. This is an irritant, the lesser the TAT, the more pleasant the user-experience.

Seamlessness: Since the last few years, Mumbai's public bus service (BEST) has introduced a pre-loaded smart card for reducing the in-bus ticketing hassle. The local railway authorities have introduced their own smart card too. However, one has to maintain two separate cards for using these services. It is not a seamless experience. Why can't Mumbai city have a common card (such as the Oyster card) that can be used 'seamlessly' across all public transport services?

Historical usage: When you are buying something on an e-commerce platform, before paying the amount, the platform suggests, 'people who bought this also bought that'. This means that the e-commerce platform is keeping a track of 'historical usage' (yours as well as that of others and has the ability to retrieve it on appropriate occasions).

All of us get alerts and notifications regarding an upcoming discount sale, a bill payment that is due in the next few days, etc. The service provider is able to do so because of their ability to track the user's past behaviour ('historical usage'). The entire analytics business is based on tracking, documenting, dicing and slicing of historical usage data.

Control to user: What would you do a decade back when you had to upgrade your laptop's operating system, say from Windows 7 to Windows 10? You would go to the local vendor, he would keep your laptop with him for a few hours, during which he would save all your existing data on another system, load the new operating system onto your laptop and then reload your data. That means the process was not under the control of the user. And many a time, at the end of it, some data would have been lost in transit.

How does the same upgrading happen today? Our devices get an 'upgrade notification' as soon as the device gets connected to a Wi-Fi network and then we can choose whether to upgrade or not, that is, 'the control has come to the user' and is no longer with the vendor (as the case was, a few years back). This is an extremely desirable attribute.

Multi-terrain usage: A SUV can be driven on a rough county road as well as on a smooth highway, that's multi-terrain usage.

Portability: How easy it is to carry the product around? This applies in case of a service too. Can you change your mobile service provider without having to change your phone number? If yes, then you have availed of mobile number 'portability'.

Disposability: Nowadays, some items are wrapped in biodegradable packaging that has seeds embedded in them. So even if you throw the wrapper around, the seeds ensure that you are greening the planet. This packaging takes care of the 'disposability' of the item. With the upcoming Electronic Waste Regulation (EWR) Act, all electronic goods manufacturers will have to integrate a supply chain that will enable disposability of the product at the end of its lifecycle.

Offline usability: Nowadays, you can watch YouTube videos or episodes on Netflix when you are offline too, provided you use the 'Make Available Offline' function.

Simplicity: Google entered the search engine business much later in the day, yet it is the most used one today, beat competition by a lot more than the proverbial mile. May I ask, what happened to Yahoo? Yahoo's home page was a mishmash of banner advertise-ments, scrolling messages, displays of multiple item categories. As against that, Google's homepage is a clean white interface with just a box where you are expected to key in your search question/ requirement. No distractions, simple and to the point. 'Simplicity' **is** the ultimate sophistication.

Optimization of functionality: Many products and services display too many functions that the user gets confused with, thus spoiling the user experience. Hence, innovators have to understand what users **really need** and optimize the functionality options.

Ease of navigation: In the late 1990s, when Nokia added the 'menu' button on its phones (remember the ones with the physical keypad), it simplified the usage. Prior to that, one had to remember the specific buttons to be pressed to enable access to various functionalities. With the introduction of the 'menu' button, Nokia eased the navigation through functionalities for the user.

Fun to use: Duolingo is a language learning app that provides the tutorial with interesting animations and graphics, making it a really enjoyable experience. It has high user traction in its category. Adding a little fun to the interface enhances the user engagement and consequently the market share.

Dynamic display of usage: Consider the following:

1. The television remote suddenly stops functioning (one of the batteries has probably died)
2. While using sketch pen, your writing/sketching begins to fade off without a warning.

On both the abovementioned occasions, you wish there had been a warning signal in advance, that is, you wished the device displayed the status of the usage dynamically

Now look at the following:

1. A transparent bottle of water. Its transparency tells me when it needs a refill.
2. Your phone's screen has a small 'battery' icon on the top end of the screen that displays the percentage of battery charge left.

Both these are examples of 'dynamic display of usage'. This reduces user-irritation while using the product.

Mode of payment: When people have multiple choices by which they can pay for a product or service that they wish to use. For example:

Pay per use: The cloud model of paying for a product/service only when you use it, without owning it, generates a much larger user base than the ownership model would have.

Pay for what you use: An intra-city cab service charges you based on the kilometers you use the service for. A tyre company is experimenting with this model, that is, one will have to pay a small upfront fee for buying a car tyre and the rest can be paid as you use the tyre on a pay per mile basis. Sensors in the car will pick up valuable information such as whether the car is being driven on a smooth freeway or a rough country road. These sensors will send the data to a cloud server and the user will be charged according to his/her usage. The kilometers that the user covers on a smooth freeway will be charged lesser per kilometer than those covered on a rough country road. Moreover, the sensors will capture the driving habits of the user and provide these to the R&D teams of the tyre manufacturer, to enable them to design better tyres.

A subscription model: Cloud services that charge you per month or per license or on a per user basis.

Use now, pay later model: Arrangements with financing partners help distribute the payments over a period of time. This captures a large user base.

In addition to the above modes of payment, there could be different methods of payment, such as through payment apps, net banking, credit/debit card, etc.

Standalone Use: Our mobile phones need to be charged repeatedly. For this, we need an external source of energy, electricity. We need to carry a paraphernalia of charges, power banks, etc., to make this possible. This means, our mobile phones are not meant for standalone use. Now, consider a calculator with photosensitive cells. The moment the calculator is exposed to any source of light, it is operational (neither do you need a charger nor a power bank). That means the 'calculator is capable of standalone use'. Imagine if our mobile phones had such photosensitive batteries. Would you not shell out at least 20 per cent extra for such a mobile phone?

Reconfigurability: When a company creates a product/service that is customizable, it has to make a lot of changes for each user. This necessitates the creation of a platform that has the ability to adapt to each user's preference. Such a platform must have the ability to reconfigure itself from user to user. Building in reconfigurability into the system architecture is a must in today's times, because consumers today are spoilt for choices and loyalty to a brand is pretty transient.

Inter-systemic component interaction: Every product/service operates in an ecosystem that comprises multiple systems and subsystems, for example, when you carry a bottle of water in a backpack, the bottle is a subsystem placed in your backpack which has your laptop and your dairy, the backpack is another subsystem having multiple components. If water from the bottle leaks out, it is bound to spoil the laptop and your dairy, that is, one component of a subsystem will interact with a component from another subsystem in a not-so-desirable manner. That is inter-systemic component interaction. A product creator has to understand this and take the necessary actions. Sometimes, this interaction may be desirable too.

Follow the below mentioned steps while using the framework:

Step 1: Identify the attributes that the user finds most relevant to the problem you are trying to solve. This would involve roping in a few consumers and seeking their inputs.

Step 2: Once a list of desirable attributes is formed, then create a 'attribute desirability quotient (ADQ)'. How to do that?

1. Ask users to rate each of the identified attributes on a scale of five on two aspects:

    a. Importance of the attribute to the user

    b. How would the user rate competing products/ brands on these attributes.

The output of this step would look as follows (for sample purposes, only seven attributes have been included in the following table). You may add columns if there are more competitors:

Sr. No.	Attributes Identified as Most Relevant (Based on User Interactions)	Importance of This Attribute to the User	Rating of Competitor #1	Rating of Competitor #2	Rating of Competitor #3
1	Capacity	4.5	3.75	2.75	3
2	Modularity	3.75	4	3.5	4
3	Affordability	4	4.25	4	3.75
4	Interoperability	4.75	3	4.25	4.25
5	Durability	4.25	3.75	4.5	4
6	Availability	4.75	4	3.5	2.75
7	Comfort	4.5	2.5	3	3

The numbers under the 'importance of this attribute to the user' column signify the 'ADQ'.

Attributes Identified as Most Relevant (Based on User Interactions)	ADQ
Capacity	4.5
Modularity	3.75
Affordability	4
Interoperability	4.75
Durability	4.25
Availability	4.75
Comfort	4.5

The difference between the 'ADQ' and the ratings of the competitors is an indication of the opportunities available in the market. If the ADQ is higher than the ratings of competing products, that's an opportunity space that can be capitalized upon before your competitors do.

It's Logical: Innovating Profitable Business Models

YOUR CHECKLIST!

1. **While creating a new product or service:** Sift through the framework and look for attributes that the user might value. Then check the relevance of these attributes for the user using the 'ADQ' as shown above.

2. **While upgrading an existing product or service:** Check for attributes that are missing from your existing product/service. Then check the relevance of these attributes for the user using the 'ADQ'.

3. **While benchmarking your product or service against competing offerings:** Check what attributes the competing products are offering, then check whether your product has those. If your customers value the attributes that your competitors have and you don't, then figure out ways in which you can integrate those into your product. At all times, keep checking the 'ADQ' with the user.

Chapter 15

The Jigsaw: Actionable Steps for Creating Breakthroughs

So far, we have seen various aspects of DK's philosophy while trying to solve a problem. Everything about that fascinates me. Once I asked him, 'Is there a process that you can define in clear, actionable steps which, if followed, will help conceptualize breakthrough solutions? And how does the process enhance the probability of making innovation happen?'

In his inimitable, nonchalant manner, DK responded, 'Well, nothing can ever be cast in concrete. Everything is relative and so is the problem-solving process. Techniques are always contextual.'

'But still, DK, with your experience of helping so many corporates and startups innovate, agnostic of what sector they operate in, you must have formulated some template', I insisted.

'Well, it is not a template, I would rather term it as a lose framework.'

I pressed on, 'DK, please elaborate, I would like to know the process that you follow. Given your strike rate, it will be highly useful for all of us.'

DK looked out from the window, overlooking the seafront of Western Mumbai and for a few moments, appeared lost. A lot seemed to be going through his mind. I could sense a feeling of discomfort creeping into his normally easy-going demeanor. Something was gnawing him deep inside. After what seemed like an eternity, his expression got back to normal. Clearing his throat, he said, 'Ok let me recount something I had been a part of almost a decade back.'

From his body language, I got a feeling that this was going to be serious stuff.

He added, 'This has nothing to do with business. I am sharing this with you since you insisted on me detailing out the process that I generally follow. This experience encompasses all the components of the process that you want to know about.'

With an uncharacteristically serious expression, he began, 'It was late evening on the 26 November 2008, I had just settled in front of the TV and was flipping through channels trying to locate where I could locate the highlights of the India–England one day international cricket series. I was very excited and eager to find it, since England had been completely blanked out in all the earlier games. Some rolling text at the bottom of the screen, on one of the channels, caught my attention. News channels were reporting incidents of random firing at CST train terminus. Then came news about more such firing at other locations. By 8.30 PM, these attacks were being reported from at least six/seven different locations. Something sinister was happening. Within the next two hours, a state of emergency had been declared and South Mumbai was under clampdown. What followed over the next 70 odd hours were unthinkable. Ten terrorists of the Lashkar-e-Taiba, a terrorist organization, based out of Pakistan, were creating mayhem across 12 different locations in South Mumbai. One seventy-two dead, three hundred plus injured and all of India shaken. Mumbai was on hold for those three days.'

'A few weeks later, me and a few like-minded students got together and decided to explore all that had happened during those fateful 70 hours and, if possible, come up with some suggestions for improving the response mechanisms of the various agencies involved. We restricted our objective to only the events during the 70 hours. We decided that we would not look into issues such as intelligence failure prior to the event, since those would be out of our reach and locus of influence.'

He continued, 'Over the next 3 months, we interacted with 200 plus people directly or indirectly involved with the events that took place on that fateful day and immediately after. The people we met comprised:

1. Folks who were trapped but survived the 70-hour ordeal
2. Folks who had managed to escape from various affected locations during those 70 hours
3. Kin of folks who lost their lives
4. Kin of folks who had survived/managed to escape
5. Security personnel who were on duty at that time
6. Ambulance drivers who ferried victims from the attack sites to hospitals
7. Medical and para-medical staff (doctors, nurses, wardboys, etc.) who attended to the injured at various government hospitals
8. Traffic cops (across hierarchies) who were on duty at that time
9. People who were at the affected locations but managed to be outside the action arena (i.e. those who were present when it all began but managed to escape before getting trapped)
10. Residents of the affected localities, who were passive witnesses

People narrated their experiences, complained about what went wrong, gave their views on what should have been and what can be done. These in-depth conversations enabled us to understand and visualize the scenarios that had unfolded then.

After painstakingly going through reams of the collected data, four categories emerged, namely

1. Escape routes
2. Response from security personnel
3. Emergency medical care
4. Rumours in the city

The important point to be noted here is that these categories emerged by themselves from the information captured, we had not begun our explorations with those categories in mind. Most of the time, while trying to solve a problem, we begin with some pre-determined categories and that's a mistake, because the information gathering process gets largely restricted. It needs to be open-ended to begin with.

Let me quickly explain how these categories emerged in an organic fashion.

ESCAPE ROUTES

Survivors who had managed to escape or survive the entire ordeal said that when they were stuck in certain buildings, they were not able to easily find directions/signages for emergency exits/refuge areas, etc. Some security guards on duty mentioned that they too were unaware of these vital locations within the buildings they were guarding. On deeper examination, we found that since the late 1990s, security had become an outsourced service. A lot of institutions had engaged external security agencies who deploy novice security guards. Most of these agencies follow a policy of rotating these guards across locations every 75 to 90 days, to avoid them getting too familiar with the inmates. As a 'good management practice (GMP)', from the security perspective this may sound right. But the lack of knowledge about the geography of the building(s) the personnel are guarding, coupled with lack of training, isn't a very good practice during such extraordinary events. They could not guide the victims either toward emergency exits or refuge areas. Findings such as these were clubbed under the category 'escape routes'.

QUICK RESPONSE FROM SECURITY PERSONNEL

The terrorists had planned the operation meticulously. They attacked different locations simultaneously beginning around 7.30 PM. Initially, the police department thought that these were stray incidents of rioting and arson and did not visualize a planned, simultaneous attack on the commercial and affluent hub of Mumbai. Their response too, was episodic rather than holistic. Mumbai had seen encounters between gangsters and cops during the 1990s. Probably on that day (26 November 2008), initially they might have thought it was something similar. The Mumbai Anti-terrorism Squad (ATS) too failed to gauge the enormity of the situation. In fact, three senior members of the ATS, hurried to one location in the same vehicle, armed with not much more than revolvers. They got shot within a few meters of each other. The terrorists were armed with sophisticated weapons. It took a few hours for the police department to piece the jigsaw together and realize the interconnected nature of these attacks. By the time the police realized the magnitude of the attacks, precious time was lost, and the terrorists had taken more or less firm control of the premises that they were holding the hostages in. Due to this, the police were unable to enter the affected locations. We were told that security folks could not get within 50–70 meters of the locations, since the terrorists had taken vantage positions within the buildings that they had stormed. Snipers had occupied windows overlooking all entrances.

EMERGENCY MEDICAL CARE

The police department declared a state of emergency about a couple of hours after the first attack. As per protocol, the emergency health care machinery whirs into action at scale, only after the police department declares a state of emergency. Victims who were trapped as hostages said that medical ambulances, etc., reached the sites a few hours after the nightmare had begun. They could not enter the premises, since the sites were under firm control of the terrorists by then. Ambulance drivers mentioned the following:

1. 'It took ages to reach the sites due to the traffic jams in the city.'

    At such times, the first thing that security agencies do is cordon off the affected areas and keep reducing the perimeter of action, to restrict the mobility of the attackers. Some roads were barricaded, leading to huge traffic snarls. Ambulance drivers complained that a distance that would normally take 15–20 minutes to cover, took almost 90. Precious minutes were lost, leading to loss of lives due to lack of medical attention.

2. Survivors being ferried in these ambulances mentioned that in a space fit for 3–4 patients, 10–12 had to be accommodated. There weren't any other options.

3. Back in 2008, there was no mandate that private hospitals accept patients in such cases of emergency. Generally, private hospitals would avoid admitting anyone related to police cases. Hence, ambulances had to be taken only to government hospitals. The nearest government was Cama Hospital, but it was invaded by two of the attackers and under their control, so no victims could be taken there. The next nearest one was Sir J. J. Hospital, which is about 5–6 km into the city. On a normal day, that distance is covered in 20 odd minutes, but that day, navigating through traffic jams, it took more than an hour. Some ambulance drivers told us that when they reached Sir J. J. Hospital, they were told that the hospital was full beyond capacity (victims were being brought in from multiple locations) and would not be able to take in more victims. They had to drive to the next closest public hospital which is B.Y. L. Nair Hospital, another 3–4 km from Sir J. J. Hospital. To cover that distance, precious minutes were lost. Some survivors told us that they witnessed the life force passing out of some who were bleeding profusely, in transit, from one hospital to another.

4. Doctors that we met, mentioned 'Victims with bullet wounds that puncture the main arteries or the abdominal region tend to bleed profusely. The discharge is almost 200–250 cc of blood/minute. The human body has about 5–5.5 litres of blood. A loss of more that 2,000–3,000 cc of blood leads to hypovolemic shock (the heart is unable to pump enough blood to the body, due to severe blood or fluid loss). Organ failure begins to set in causing irreparable damage', that is, even if an individual is infused with blood after having lost more than 2,000–3,000 cc, she/he may not be able to be

resuscitated. So, if you calculate the time window (from the time of injury) for blood infusion to take place, it is about 10–15 minutes. At best, application of pressure with cloth, sterile bandages, etc., could stretch it to 25–30 minutes. That means a patient has to receive an infusion within 25–30 minutes of sustaining a potentially fatal bullet wound.

5. Para-medical staff on duty claimed they fell incredibly short on the infrastructure front.

   a. They couldn't test blood groups quickly enough. Victims were being brought in at a rate they were not equipped to handle.

   b. Even after testing victims for their blood groups, some died due to specific blood groups not being available in the in-house blood banks.

   c. All of this had happened post 7.00 PM, hence all senior doctors had left for the day. Only the resident doctors (who are mostly junior in the hierarchy) were available. The same applied for nursing and other para-medical staff. The seniors generally opt for the day shift, leaving the juniors in charge for the night. The hospitals were operating at about 60–70 per cent of their capacity with less-experienced personnel. There was no way they could cope with the inflow of victims that later increased to almost 300 per cent of capacity.

All these findings were clubbed under the category, 'emergency medical care'.

RUMOURS IN THE CITY

As the news of the attacks began to spread, news channels began airing the details leading to panic among citizens. TV anchors, with their penchant for theatrics and drama added fuel by airing their conjectures as 'the reality'. Once the police declared a state of emergency, all mobile service providers were ordered to jam their networks in order to prevent random rumours from being spread. However, kin of people who were stuck at the affected sites said that, they got a couple of calls from their kin and then there was total silence due to the mobile networks being jammed. Sitting at home, with no knowledge about the status of their kin, their minds began to spin doomsday scenarios. At such times, deadly canards began making the rounds. One such rumour was that Mumbai would soon be bombed by the Pakistani Air Force. In fact, during our interactions, we met five families that had gathered their belongings, jumped into their cars and left Mumbai from the Northern exits of the city.

All such findings were clubbed under the category, 'rumours in the city'.

DK paused for a while. He wanted to continue talking, but his emotions were getting the better of him. His voice was giving him away.

Sipping on a glass of water, he continued, 'The "categorization of the findings helped us define the problems precisely". Now, I will explain the further process we followed, by picking up one category as a sample. Let's pick up emergency medical care as the category to demonstrate the steps we followed.

'The next step is to correctly identify the problems and then state ideal situations to overcome the problem.' The following will make it clear to you:

Sr. No.	Problem Identified	Ideal Situation
1	Ambulances were stuck in traffic jams leading to delays in treatment	An ambulance carrying the injured **should not encounter traffic**
2	Some hospitals could not take in victims due to overcrowding	**No hospital should refuse admission** at such times of emergency
3	Precious time was lost for blood group identification	There **should be no delay in blood group identification**

Sr. No.	Problem Identified	Ideal Situation
4	Blood of some types (blood groups) was unavailable	There should be **no shortage of blood**
5	Shortage of medical/para-medical staff	Medical and paramedical staff **should be available at all times**

'The statements that capture the ideal situations are actually the attributes of the final solutions. In other words, the ideal situations are criteria that the final solution must meet.'

Being able to formulate this list is the crux of problem solving. If you can do that, half the solution is already in place.

Now, the next task is to generate ideas to meet these criteria. This is where you have to let your imagination take over, no idea is silly. You must warn your team members that they should not scoff at each other's ideas, however silly those might sound. Because each one will have a different perspective and it is important that the team builds on these wild thoughts. 'These flights of fancy actually are the genesis of breakthroughs. It is here that paradigm shifts occur.'

Let me tell you, in brief, how we moved ahead.

There are multiple triggers for ideation. One of my favorite techniques is:

'Looking for inspirations/analogies from some unrelated domains or from nature'

Why is this my favourite? Because I genuinely believe that there is no idea/solution that is original in this world. Any idea that seems original is a cut-copy-paste version of something that has already been solved somewhere else. It is the limitation of our mind that fails to see the connections. We have to open our minds to connect the dots.

As a team, we then began to look for analogies. We did this by picking one statement at a time, from the list:

Meeting Criteria #1: An ambulance carrying the injured **should not encounter traffic.**

Imagine situations where there is absolutely no blockage, everything moves seamlessly, for example, air, water, etc., after discussing for some time 'we narrowed down on an analogical situation wherein if an "ultra-high level VIP visits a city–how smoothly the traffic is managed then".' There are set protocols that are followed. Can similar protocols be followed at times of unprecedented emergencies as such attacks? This was the question we needed to answer. On further exploration, we discovered the following protocols followed back in 2008:

When an ultra-high-level VIP would be on the streets with her/his convoy:

1. There would be continuous monitoring of the traffic situation and constant updates would be exchanged between the navigator in the lead car and the traffic control room.

2. There used to a be a tab in the navigator's car, back then. Information about the traffic situation would be displayed on these tabs. Remember back then (in 2008–2009), there were no Google Maps with red and blue lines, as we have today.

3. In case of an ultra-high-level VIP, the route is never kept predictable (to avoid any pre-planned attack). In fact, 3–4 pre-planned contingency routes are always kept open. But anything that is pre-planned is subject to an attack. The navigator of such VIPs is a highly trusted individual, who can take a decision (at the last moment) to change the route, if she/he smells something fishy ahead. She/he has the authority to take a completely new route in such situations. This means, a fifth route (a totally unplanned one) needs to be cleared by the police department. Is there a protocol to be able to do that? Yes, the traffic police department does have a standard operating procedure to make this happen on the fly.

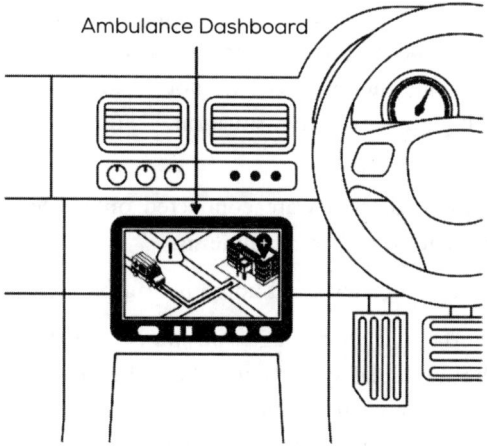

a. At the press of a button, from the control room, all the through signals on the fifth route become green and cross signals become red. This means, all the traffic on the route ahead is made to pass faster and the cross-traffic that would block intersections, made to stop, creating a fast corridor for the VIP convoy to pass.

b. Moreover, a wireless message gets relayed to all the traffic cops manning those intersections to let through traffic pass by and cross-traffic be held.

To meet criteria # 1, our suggestion was 'A dashboard (as shown in Figure 15.1) with all traffic information should be available in an ambulance.' This would empower the ambulance driver to avoid crowded routes.

Meeting criteria #2: No hospital should refuse admission at such times of emergency.

Subsequent to looking for multiple analogies, 'we narrowed down on Expedia.com, the hotel-booking aggregator as the analogy.' Back in 2009, Expedia had begun to gain popularity in India. The one thing that fascinated me about Expedia was that whatever travel dates you mention and ask Expedia to show the availability of hotels at your destination, does it ever say, 'No accommodation available'? It always throws up at least a hundred options. That means, it never refuses admission to anyone who visits their site. How does Expedia manage to do it? If they can, then why can we not borrow that protocol from them and use it in the emergency situation. To find more, we explored how Expedia operates:

1. All hotel databases are connected onto one platform and information is shared seamlessly.

2. Latest occupancy of all hotels is available in real time.

To meet criteria # 2, our suggestion was, 'The dashboard in the ambulance should display information about the latest occupancy at all hospitals in the vicinity in real time (as shown in Figure 15.2), along with the route map to the hospital.' This would enable the ambulance driver to take the injured to the right hospital, where admission would **not** be refused.

Figure 15.2. Dashboard in Ambulance, Displaying Bed Availability in Hospitals in Real Time

HOSPITALS IN ROUTE	AVAILABLE BEDS
● Sir. JJ Hospital	72
○ Lokmanya Tilak	19
○ Dr. Tata Memorial	43
○ Government	55
○ King Edward Memorial	1
○ Kasturba Hospital	32
○ Gokuldas Tejpal	115
○ Saifee	52
○ Seth V.C. Gandhi	13
○ M.A Vora Municipal	0

It's Logical: Innovating Profitable Business Models

Meeting criteria #3: There should be **no delay in blood group identification**.

'The analogy we used was, 'How does an ETC tag work at a toll booth?'

1. The camera scans the tag on the car, that is, there is instantaneous identification with the use of radio-frequency identification (RFID) technology

2. A signal is sent to the payment gateway, that is, there is immediate data transfer

3. The payment gateway debits the concerned account and sends a signal back to the toll gate which opens up and the car passes through seamlessly, that is, there is instantaneous updation.

All this happens when the car is moving at a speed of about 5–10 km/hr. It doesn't have to stop, everything happens absolutely seamlessly, so can this process not be adopted for eliminating the 'delay in blood group identification'?

To meet criteria # 3, we suggested:

1. 'The paramedic in the ambulance should have kits for instant blood group identification.

2. There should be an encoder in every ambulance. When each victim's blood group is recorded into this encoder, it would generate an RFID tag (with the blood group information encoded into it) and the respective victim would be tagged in the ambulance itself. Thus, saving precious seconds.'

Initially, we thought that the tag generated from the encoder should be in the form of a wristband. However, when we shared this idea with a few doctors, they said, 'In this case, you are attending to victims of gunshot wounds, but if some other time you are attending to bomb blast victims, some victims may have their limbs sheared off, the wrist band won't work.' Our team huddled in and came up with another possibility of generating the tags in the form of a sticker that could be stuck anywhere on the body of the victim. The doctors intervened

Figure 15.3. Tag with Blood Group Information Encoded

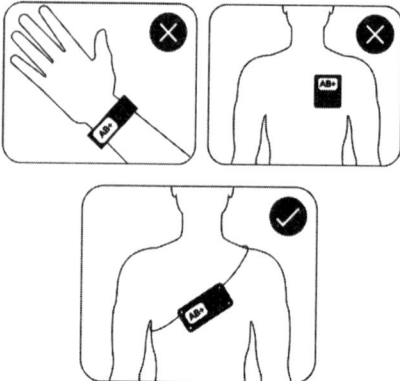

again, 'In case of violent injuries, in addition to blood, a lot of body fluids ooze out of the body, it is virtually impossible to stick anything on the victim's clothing.'

Finally, we suggested a very crude solution: The tag generated should have pre-punched holes at the edges and we would keep long twines (one meter in length) in the ambulance, such that the tag could be tied around any part of the body (as depicted in Figure 15.3).

Meeting criteria #4: There should be **no shortage of blood (of any group).**

Here, 'we used the analogy that 'In case of a war, the armed forces ensure that there is never a shortage of ammunition at the warfront.'

How is this managed? We had to find answers to this question. There are standard protocols to overcome any shortfall of ammunition.

1. Continuous updates of stocks of ammunition at the warfront are communicated to the nearest warehouse.

2. All warehouses in the country are electronically connected to each other and they share information about available stock in real time.

3. Immediate logistics are arranged to take care of shortfalls at the warfront.

To meet criteria #4, drawing from these protocols, we suggested:

1. 'Information about the blood groups should be instantly communicated from the ambulance to the hospital(s).

2. The hospital should have an updated record of the stocks in all blood banks in its immediate surroundings as well as the city. Blood banks in the city should be connected on a common platform and share information about their respective stocks (volumes and types of blood groups).

3. If a particular type of blood group is unavailable, then it should be brought in (from the respective blood bank), so that it reaches the respective hospital, before the ambulance does.' (Using the SOPs laid down for the ambulance's route management).

Information coming in from various ambulances would be captured onto one platform. This data would provide information about the type of blood and approximate quantity required for every injured individual. Refer to Figure 15.4 for the information dashboard visible to the hospital staff.

All blood banks in the city being connected electronically onto a platform would ensure that the hospital would have access to blood groups that may not be available in their in-house blood banks. With a continuous feed coming in from the ambulances about the types of blood groups required, the hospital staff would know what blood groups are required. If the hospital did not have any type of blood group required, then immediate logistics would have to be arranged at the backend (use of SOPs to meet criteria #1 would be used therein).

Meeting criteria #5: Medical and paramedical staff **should be available at all times**.

The analogy that we used for this will bring a smile on your face. For all the earlier four analogies, we discussed and debated for a long while, before reaching a consensus. But this one that someone suggested, and we all agreed at once.

Figure 15.4. Dashboard at the Hospital End Displaying Blood Availability Versus Requirement

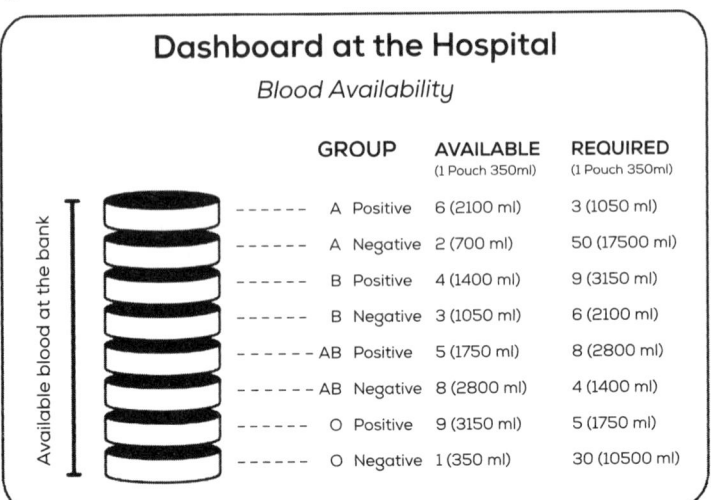

Dashboard at the Hospital
Blood Availability

	GROUP		AVAILABLE (1 Pouch 350ml)	REQUIRED (1 Pouch 350ml)
– – – – – –	A	Positive	6 (2100 ml)	3 (1050 ml)
– – – – – –	A	Negative	2 (700 ml)	50 (17500 ml)
– – – – – –	B	Positive	4 (1400 ml)	9 (3150 ml)
– – – – –	B	Negative	3 (1050 ml)	6 (2100 ml)
– – – – – –	AB	Positive	5 (1750 ml)	8 (2800 ml)
– – – – – –	AB	Negative	8 (2800 ml)	4 (1400 ml)
– – – – – –	O	Positive	9 (3150 ml)	5 (1750 ml)
– – – – – –	O	Negative	1 (350 ml)	30 (10500 ml)

Available blood at the bank

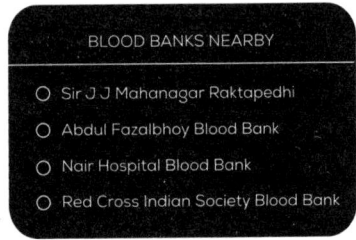

BLOOD BANKS NEARBY

O Sir J J Mahanagar Raktapedhi
O Abdul Fazalbhoy Blood Bank
O Nair Hospital Blood Bank
O Red Cross Indian Society Blood Bank

As kids, we all have done this a few times. We would call up our mom, say at eight in the evening and rightfully tell her, 'Mom, I am with 10 of my friends and we are famished, will be home for dinner with them by 9.' Over the phone, she would give us an earful, but when the gang reached home by 9:30 PM, everything would be laid out on the table ready to be gorged upon. Haven't we all been through this some time or the other?

'So, "how does mom ensure availability of food at all times" under such tight constraints?' This was the analogy that we used for meeting criteria #5.

After speaking to a few moms of teenagers, we realized that they have an algorithm in their minds and a protocol of activities to

It's Logical: Innovating Profitable Business Models

Figure 15.5. Alerts to the Pre-registered Medics/Para-Medics

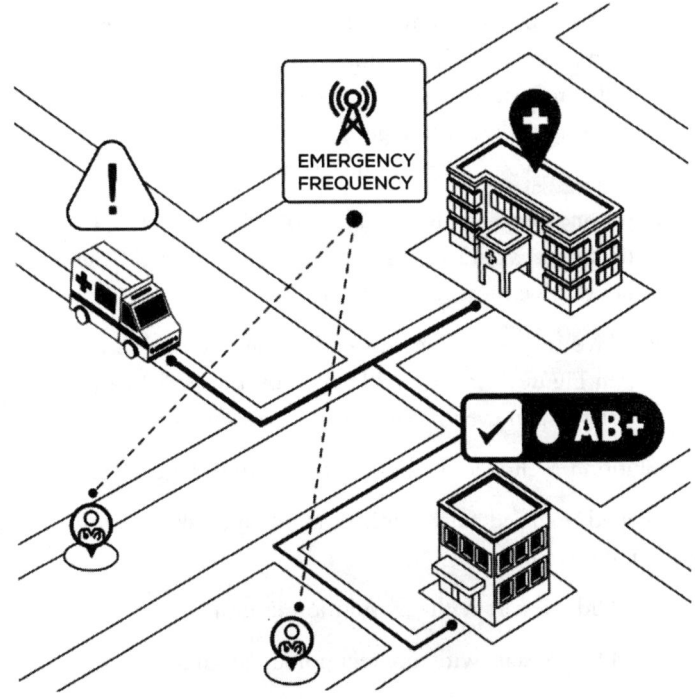

manage such situations. We decoded that and came to the following conclusions:

1. Mom checks all stock in the refrigerator and kitchen cabinets

2. If there is a shortage, then she connects with neighbours

3. If neighbours are not available, then, as a last resort, calls up the local restaurant or 24/7 options such as Dominos, Pizza Hut, etc.

The last point of the 24x7 food service options, triggered an idea that we must have a similar option for medical and para-medical staff too.

To meet criteria # 5, we suggested:

1. 'We must have a repository of medical/paramedical staff (private, as well as government hospital employees) who

should be **pre-registered**, with a pledge that they would make themselves available at short notice, at times of such emergencies. Their contact details would be available on this repository and the moment an emergency situation is declared; they would get a text message asking them to make themselves available at the required hospital.'

However, one problem that was unsolved was that if the mobile service networks would be jammed, then how would the medics/paramedics receive these text messages.

2. 'We suggested that this entire communication (as depicted in Figure 15.5) should happen over a special frequency that stays open even if regular networks are blocked.'

The solution timeline looked like that shown in Figure 15.6.

DK stopped, exhaled fully, looked at me and asked, 'Now, I have three questions for you:

1. Did we start with any solution in mind?

2. Did we start with any technology in mind?

3. Did we invent any technology?'

I responded, 'No'.

He continued, 'Normally, when we solve a problem, invariably we start with a rough solution in mind or we start with a premise that we will use a particular technology, don't we? But here you must have realized that we didn't do that. We followed a broad framework and adopted appropriate technologies at the right times. This is what I mean by 'user first, technology later'.

He smiled, looked at me in the eye and continued, 'Now to answer your question, is there a process that I follow? Let me summarize what we did at that time.

Step 0: Map the ecosystem—200+ 'interactions with every stakeholder involved'.

Figure 15.6. The Solution as a Timeline

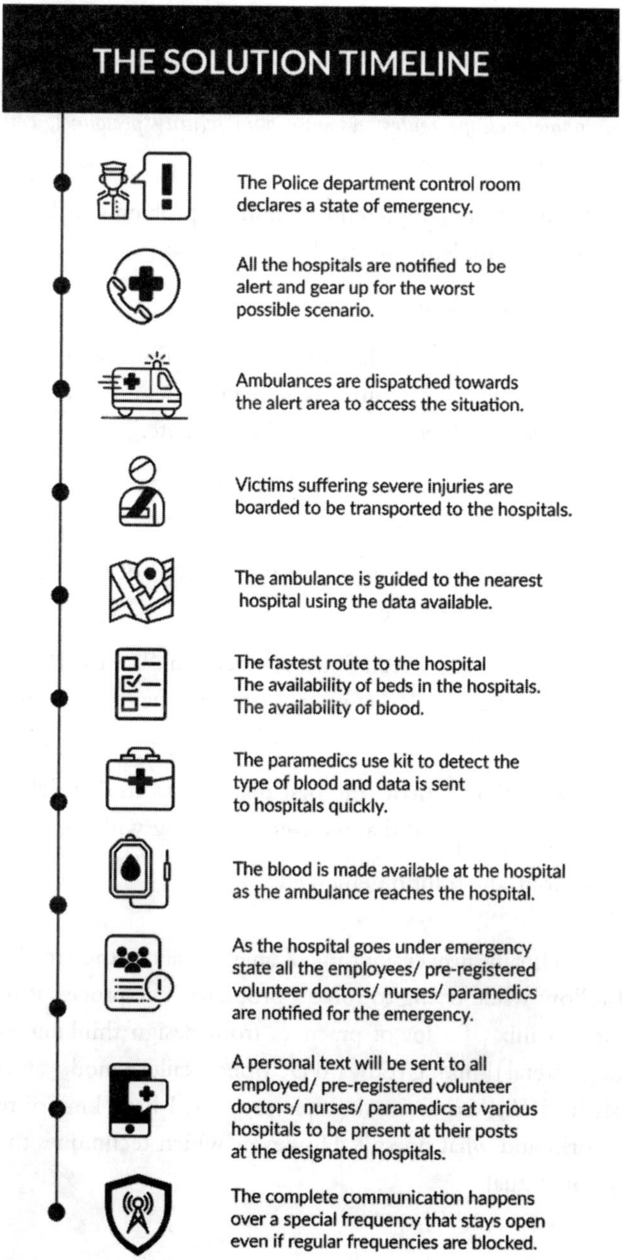

THE SOLUTION TIMELINE

The Police department control room declares a state of emergency.

All the hospitals are notified to be alert and gear up for the worst possible scenario.

Ambulances are dispatched towards the alert area to access the situation.

Victims suffering severe injuries are boarded to be transported to the hospitals.

The ambulance is guided to the nearest hospital using the data available.

The fastest route to the hospital
The availability of beds in the hospitals.
The availability of blood.

The paramedics use kit to detect the type of blood and data is sent to hospitals quickly.

The blood is made available at the hospital as the ambulance reaches the hospital.

As the hospital goes under emergency state all the employees/ pre-registered volunteer doctors/ nurses/ paramedics are notified for the emergency.

A personal text will be sent to all employed/ pre-registered volunteer doctors/ nurses/ paramedics at various hospitals to be present at their posts at the designated hospitals.

The complete communication happens over a special frequency that stays open even if regular frequencies are blocked.

Step 1: Collected all our findings

Step 2: Looked at all of them together– 'without any bias'.

Step 3: Some connections and affinities emerged organically *(categories emerged, namely escape routes, response from security personnel, emergency medical care, rumours in the city).*

Step 4: Each category represented multiple problems to be solved– 'clearly defined problems emerged'.

Step 5: We then took one category at a time.

Step 6: Then we stated what the ideal situations should be: 'An ambulance carrying the injured should not encounter traffic, there should no delay in blood group identification, etc.'

Step 7: The ideal situations firmly formed the criteria that the final solution must meet.

Step 8: For each ideal situation, we then delved deeper to generate ideas to make them possible.

Here one can use various techniques for ideation. 'We used "Analogies from unrelated domains", that is, how similar issues have been tackled in different domains.'

Step 9: We explored '**how**' the best practices from that field can be adopted for the problems that we were grappling with.

Lo and behold, the solution emerged.

These steps finally answer your initial question about the broad process that I follow while trying to solve a problem. The process is nothing new, it is a mix of a lot of practices from design thinking, systems thinking, lateral thinking (Edward De Bono), failure modes and effects analysis (FMEA), etc. Over multiple projects, I have kind of realized what works and what doesn't. However, which techniques to use, is highly contextual.'

 It's Logical: Innovating Profitable Business Models

IMPRESSIVE IMPRESSIONS

1. 'There is a broad process, which, if followed, can lead us to the creation of breakthrough concepts.' Throughout the process, in the above instance, DK's constant endeavor was to 'keep the user at the centre', be it the ambulance driver, the paramedic in the ambulance, the hospital staff at the blood bank or the injured victim. This enabled him and his team to conceptualize a holistic system of micro-solutions for every problem.

2. 'The in-depth stakeholder analysis' helped bring out multiple facets of the situation and then each of these stakeholders were spoken to and their opinions weighed in. This 'enabled the problems to be articulated very clearly'. Once this happens, finding solutions is not too far.

3. 'The categories, in which the various issues fall, should emerge organically', that is, the information should speak to you. One should not begin the stakeholder exploration with pre-meditated categories (most of the time, problem solvers make this mistake). By letting the emerging information fall into categories organically, one remains objective, unbiased and true to the issues involved.

4. 'While visualizing the ideal situations, no constraints were brought into the picture.' The ideal situations envisaged were direct reflections of the tightly defined problem statements. Here, one should adopt the '**possibility first, feasibility later approach**'.

5. During the idea-generation phase, team members 'must pledge not to scoff at any flights of fancy' displayed by their colleagues. The team charter should have a clause stating, 'We will build on each other's ideas and not puncture holes in them at the beginning. Operational feasibilities will be thought about later.'

6. 'Reinventing the wheel is not necessary. Looking at analogies from unrelated domains or from nature is a powerful trigger

for idea generation.' If the problems are defined correctly, then the essence of these problems have solutions outside the domain. It is up to us to open our minds and connect the unconnected dots.

7. **Do not begin the problem-solving process with a solution in mind.** When that happens, one is only trying to validate that all the time. Objectivity is totally lost.

8. Avoid bringing technology in the picture too early. 'Let the right technologies emerge at the appropriate times, to solve well-defined user problems.'

Chapter 16

Suturing: The Common Sense behind Business Model Innovation

Through the previous chapters, we got a glimpse into DK's various unconventional, yet logical lenses. Now, it is time to sew it all up into an actionable framework that all of us can use in our day-to-day functioning, on the professional as well as personal front.

1. We began by dissecting 'how some companies created win-win situations in their respective business domains and disrupted entrenched incumbents.' DK's research on businesses that outimagined competition by creating unique business models and not just innovating on products and technologies, demonstrates this in detail.

2. Envisaging the ecosystem through in-depth stakeholder mapping at the outset, lays a strong foundation for things to follow. It helps in opening up multiple perspectives to the same problem. It enables visualizing win-win situations while crystalizing business models later.

3. DK's emphasis on establishing 'last mile user connect' will enable companies get things 'first time right'. When you get things right the first time, you are able to save hugely on budgets and time over-runs and the subsequent heart burn. Time spent with users at the beginning is time saved later in making course corrections. This is true for large corporates as well as startups who run on shoestring funding. Establishing 'last mile user connect', reduces the time for

any product/service launch. Companies are waking up to this fact.

4. For understanding the user:

    a. 'User first, technology later' has been DK's mantra throughout.

    b. 'Gamification as a tool for user research is extremely effective as it reflects the **real choice/preference of the user.**'

    c. 'Getting the bull's-eye question': Try to identify that one question that captures the essence of your user research.

    d. Immersive ethnography: User research has to happen where the action is. 'Contextualize' your user research. Ensure that user research is carried out in the reality of the consumer. If, for any reason, it is not possible to be in the actual setting, get as close to it as possible through creative simulation.

    e. Use memetics to uncover trends in society. 'Memetics helps identify some common stimuli to trigger specific responses.'

    f. 'Define your business from the user's perspective, not yours'.

    g. 'Do not just sell what you make. Try to make what might sell'.

5. 'DK's cheat sheet on new product creation' would help identify certain attributes that one might have missed while conceptualizing a product or a service

    a. The 'attribute desirability quotient (ADQ)' can be used effectively in the following situations:

        i. While creating a new product or service

        ii. While upgrading an existing product or service

        iii. While benchmarking your product or service against competing offerings

All the above will help conceptualize some great products or services. But for that offering to be successful in the market, one has to create a unique and sustainable business model. We experienced the magic of business model innovation in Chapter 2.

It's always nice to hear stories about successful ventures, understand underlying reasons for the success and feel good about having learnt something new. But the tough part is how to apply that learning to make sense in one's own situation.

So, the question that needs an answer is:

How does one create unique business models? 'Is there a template that one can use?'

I will share something that DK has used extensively while consulting with large corporates as well as startups and it has always worked. It is so simple that one may ignore it as common sense. But everything profound, is simple to understand, isn't it? Well, it may be simple to understand but definitely not easy to act upon. Therein lies the key to successful execution. Keep it simple but be extremely diligent in executing it. Whenever, DK looks at how to structure a business model for a venture, he asks the six questions illustrated in Figure 16.1.

Figure 16.1. 5H–1W Framework for Business Model Innovation

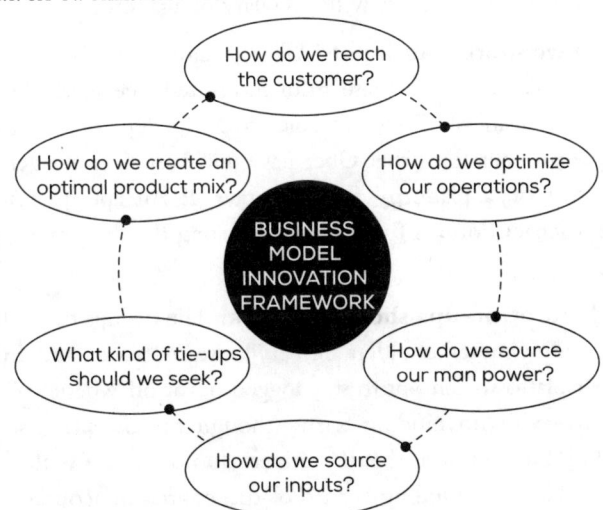

Rather than explaining the above questions through semantics, DK prefers to use an example.

In the second chapter, we discussed how Uber disrupted the industry with its unique business model. Let us apply the above framework to Uber.

How do we optimize our operations? Uber identified the non-value-adding assets of the fleet rental companies and created a service whereby the fleet rental companies could monetize their idle assets and Uber earned a commission on the same. Due to this, Uber does business with **zero inventory** of its own. That enables Uber to run their operations with minimal staff and minimal real estate.

How do we source our manpower? Initially, their manpower comprised the drivers employed by the fleet rental companies. Later on, as Uber grew, Uber extended the same model to individual cab owners, by promising them good business. By doing so, Uber actually captured a large number of freelancers, with no fixed commitment, thus minimizing their own sunk costs. The 'employee' cost for Uber is almost entirely variable (except for their management and support staff). In fact, their drivers are entrepreneurs themselves with the drive to make as much money as possible using the Uber platform. So, Uber has a motivated workforce, with no salary obligations.

How do we source our inputs? Uber's major inputs are the vehicles. They are able to source these from motivated freelancers (with the promise of business). They are able to do so due to the nature of the aggregator platform that Uber has built. Remember 'aggregating competitors on a platform' from Chapter 2? An apt application of one of Michael Porter's five forces—reducing the 'bargaining power of suppliers'.

What kind of tie-ups should we seek? The tie-ups that Uber has with its supplying stakeholders are very loose contracts. The driver on the Uber platform can opt to stay logged on or off whenever he/she wishes to, with no binding terms (though the incentive structure created by Uber ensures that the drivers do not log off without solid reasons). The non-binding nature of the contract encourages more drivers to hook onto the Uber platform, due to the win-win nature of the arrangement.

How do we create an optimal product mix? Uber started with only luxury cars. Gradually, they discovered that the service was appreciated in every demographic of the population and launched their most popular service UberGo. Over the years, they have added Uber Pool, Uber Hire services too. Uber Pool enables cost-conscious passengers to save money by offering the option of sharing their ride with someone. Uber Hire enables a passenger to hire the vehicle for the entire day (minimum of eight hours a day). Of late, they have added inter-city services too. With this, they have captured the entire spectrum of passengers, cutting across all demographics.

How do we reach the customer? In the pre-Uber days, a person wanting to commute, would go out in search of a cab. Uber took the headache and discomfort out of that experience and made it very simple and convenient. The app geo-locates the prospective passenger and available cabs around her/his location and matches one cab with the passenger. The cab comes to the user at her/his doorstep, that is, the service comes to the customer and not vice versa, which used to be the case (causing inconvenience to the customer). That's how Uber reaches its customer in a simple and efficient manner. Existing users are given referral codes which can be used to invite their friends to use the Uber platform. The person referring a new user is incentivized by Uber. Uber has many different ways of reaching out to prospective users.

That's how simple the 5H–1W framework is. The questions are very straightforward, however each one needs a lot of thinking to answer. Do try it on your company's existing business model or when you are trying to disrupt an existing one.

Before I sign off, remember: Define your business from the user's perspective and you will always remain relevant. In addition, you will constantly keep innovating.

Epilogue

I hope I have been able to break the myth, 'innovation is akin to rocket science', that a majority of us fall prey to. Oftentimes, we think we are ill-equipped or incapable of creating breakthroughs. The purpose of this book is to prove, with concrete examples, that with a sensible head on one's shoulders and relentless focus on the user, 'anyone' can become innovative.

As a business professional, one has to develop the ability to not just spot opportunities for oneself or one's own business, but to explore and examine how one can create win-win situations for the various players in the ecosystem. Unless, we create 'win-win situations', we 'cannot' create sustainable business models. If there are entities that are at loggerheads with one another, the business model is bound to crumble sooner or later. The earlier one figures out how to create win-win situations, the better the sustainability of the business. This has to be embedded into our thinking. The leadership of companies must make this an important part of their capability-building agenda.

Many a time, I get asked, 'So you liken business to charity or philanthropy?' I would rather refer to it as 'enlightened self-interest'. When one rises above the tunnel vision of self-interest and becomes aware of the fact there are other stakeholders who have an interest in your well-being and so should you have in theirs, one begins to move towards 'enlightened self-interest'. When we have a critical mass of corporate executives who think through the lens of 'enlightened self-interest', we will be able to create unique and sustainable business models. I sincerely believe it is really not that difficult to raise our thinking to a slightly higher plane of thinking.

Is this a new concept?

वसुधैव कुटुम्बकम—literally translated, it means, 'The entire Earth is one family.'

It's an ancient concept from Indian philosophy. It shouldn't be alien to us. This concept directly translates into empathy, which is the latest buzz word doing the rounds in management circles. Is it really new to us Indians? 'Relentless user-focus' is a natural extension of this concept. And therein lies the 'genesis of innovation'. So where are we missing out?

Here is where our education system comes into the picture. At primary and high-school levels, our children get evaluated based not on their ability to express their views and opinions but on their ability to choose the right answer from a limited number of options. A look at the kinds of evaluation systems employed at school levels reveals that a large percentage of evaluation happens through multiple choice questions (MCQs). This enables automation of the evaluation process. Automating the evaluation process does ensure uniform grading standards, but does it foster deeper exploration of a topic? It does not. We are bringing up our children with the mindset that there is only one solution to a problem. We have to help our children move away from this binary view of the world because real life happens to be otherwise. Life is myriad of multiple perspectives. MCQ-based evaluation is not helping our children understand this mosaic. While this (MCQ-based evaluation) may work for exact sciences, it is completely out of place for topics which need perspectives from multiple angles. The current education system, with a few exceptions, is absolutely incapable of opening the minds of our children to multiple perspectives. Therein lies the reason of an individual with a 'low empathy quotient'. So how will our children develop this ability? Unless, they develop this ability, we will always be short of innovators and original thinkers. I am convinced, 'Education doesn't need a rethink, it needs a "total revamp".' Being a product of an inadequate education system doesn't mean we have to continue to see the world as black and white. It is a mindset that can be changed. As soon as we are awakened to the acceptance that there are no absolutes, but different shades of color to every perspective. The awakening can happen anytime. Opening our minds to different perspectives can be triggered through the simplest of means. Are we open to them?

This book is an attempt to help us move in that direction.

About the Author

Dr Kaustubh Dhargalkar is an entrepreneur-turned-academician, innovation evangelist and startup mentor. He founded three companies from 1990 to 2005 in the domain of productivity-enhancement technologies for manufacturing. Exited all his companies in 2005, took a year off to learn the science of Yoga. He holds a PhD in corporate innovation and design thinking. Currently, Kaustubh works with large corporates (HP, Daimler India, Citibank, Mahindra Group, Capgemini, Honeywell, Eaton, etc.) on 'how to enhance the innovation quotient'. He trains executives in design thinking and breakthrough concept creation. His views on innovation and strategy are sought by publications such as Knowledge@Wharton, *Springer*, *Engineering & Technology* (E&T) Europe, etc.

Kaustubh has been recognized as the top seven global innovators at the Smart City Expo World Congress, Barcelona 2015, for his paper titled, 'A collaborative business model for reducing the REAL carbon footprint of electric vehicles'.

He has been 'a runner-up at the Wharton School's prestigious Global Innovation Tournament' in 2010. He has two TEDx talks to his credit. He has trained more than 5,500 individuals over 50,000 plus hours of training in the space of design thinking, creative problem-solving, breakthrough ideation, disruptive business models for emerging technologies, etc.

A teacher at heart, Kaustubh is a sought-after visiting faculty at IIT Bombay, ICT Mumbai (formerly known as University Department of Chemical Technology [UDCT]), IIM Sirmaur, Narsee Monjee Institute of Management Studies (NMIMS), WE School, etc. He has been a mentor at various startup incubators across the country, notable among them are the Centre for Innovation, Incubation and Enterprise at IIM Ahmedabad, Wadhwani Foundation-National Entrepreneurship

Network (WF-NEN), Catalyst at IIT Mandi, Zone Startups, etc., and has mentored more than 150 startups over the last decade, helping them scale by building robust business models.

He is the recipient of the Entrepreneurship Educator and Mentor Award by the Ministry of Skill Development and Entrepreneurship—Government of India—jointly with Intel, British Council, Entrepreneurship Development Institute of India (EDII) and NEN in March 2015.

He has been featured as a 'changemaker' on the Dr Subhash Chandra Show (Zee Business) in June 2017.[1]

He is a trained yoga instructor too. His sessions on meditation and *pranayama* are highly sought after at AMI Yoga (Chembur, Mumbai).

---

[1] https://www.youtube.com/watch?v=EZGd7Clz0xE